Anonymous

Food for thinking Christians

Why evil was permitted and kindred topics

Anonymous

Food for thinking Christians
Why evil was permitted and kindred topics

ISBN/EAN: 9783337201265

Printed in Europe, USA, Canada, Australia, Japan

Cover: Foto ©Lupo / pixelio.de

More available books at **www.hansebooks.com**

FOR

THINKING CHRISTIANS.

WHY EVIL

WAS

PERMITTED

AND

KINDRED TOPICS.

"To make all see, what is the fellowship of the mystery, which from the beginning of the world hath been hid in God." "Wherein he hath abounded toward us in all wisdom and prudence; having made known unto us the mystery of his will, according to his good pleasure which he hath purposed in himself:—that in the dispensation of the fullness of times, he might gather together in one, all things in Christ." Eph. i, 8, and iii, 4, 5, 9.

FREE SUPPLEMENT

TO

"ZION'S WATCH TOWER,"

PITTSBURGH, PA.

1881.

PREFACE.

THE design of this pamphlet is, first, to supply to such Christians as are alive and fully consecrated, and hungering and thirsting after a fuller knowledge of "Our Father" and his plans, what we believe to be "meat in due season;" leading such to perform all their consecration vows: secondly, to awaken those who are *asleep* in Zion—showing those who are not truth-hungry, what they are too much occupied with worldly plans to know, viz., that they are starving for the "good word of God," though they say— We are "rich and increased in goods and have need of nothing."

"I love to tell the Story!
More wonderful it seems,
Than all the golden fancies
Of all our golden dreams:
I love to tell the Story!
It did so much for me;
And that is just the reason
I tell it now to thee."

It is our part, under heavenly direction, to thus scatter the food—the seeds of thoughts; it is God's part to water and give the increase—in some thirty, some sixty, and in some a hundred-fold to his praise. We leave the results with him.

ZION'S WATCH TOWER.

PART I.

WHY EVIL WAS PERMITTED.

A DIALOGUE.

B.—GOOD evening, Brother *A.*: if you are at leisure I would like to have some conversation with reference to the Bible.

A.—I am at leisure, my brother, and such a conversation should be of interest and profit to both of us. Have you struck a new vein of precious metal in the mine of truth?

B.—Well, no; I cannot say so. The fact is, I am somewhat perplexed to know whether the Bible is really a mine of truth or not. There are many beautiful truths taught in the Bible which commend themselves to my judgment, and if I could only have my mind clear on some points, I would gladly accept the whole. It seems, too, that there must be some way out of my difficulties, if I could only find it, for surely the book is stamped with a wisdom higher than human, and my difficulty may arise from a failure to comprehend it more fully.

A.—Well, my brother, it gives me great pleasure to meet with an honest inquirer after truth. You are anxious, then, to find the connecting links in the great chain which binds the interests of humanity to the throne of God. We believe that all Scripture is given by inspiration of God, and that the Spirit will guide us in the understanding of it. If it should please him to use me as his mouth-piece it will be a great privilege and if I can render any assistance it will afford me pleasure.

B.—Well, can you explain why evil was permitted? If God is infinite in power, wisdom, and goodness, why did he permit his fair creation to be so marred by sin? After creating our first parents perfect and upright, why did he permit Satan to present the temptation, or why allow the forbidden tree to have a place among the good? Could he not have prevented all possibility of man's overthrow?

A.—I see just where your difficulty lies, and I think I can make it very plain to you. It pleased God for the joy it gives him to dispense his goodness, and to exercise the attributes of his glorious being, to create various orders of intelligent beings. Some he has endowed with greater capacity than others; but each he made perfectly adapted to his sphere. We are acquainted with many forms of life in our world, but above all others stands man, the masterpiece of God's workmanship, endowed with reason and intelligence superior to all others, and given the dominion over all. He was made upright and perfect; God pronounced him "very good"—a perfect man—physically, mentally, and morally, yet unacquainted with evil and lacking experience. Had evil never been placed before him he could not have resisted it, and consequently there would have been no virtue nor merit in his right-doing. I presume I need scarcely remark here that not the fruit of the tree but the act of disobedience caused man's fall.

B.—But could not God have made man unchangeably perfect?

A.—No; to have done so would have been to make another God. Unchangeableness is an attribute only of an infallible, infinite being—God. He who cannot err must, of necessity, be all-wise, all-powerful, and consequently eternal.

B.—I had never thought of it so.

A.—If an intelligent being is to be made at all, he must be made liable to change; and, as he was created pure, any change must be from purity to sin. He could not even know the meaning of *good* unless he had *evil* to contrast with it. He could not be reckoned as obedient to God unless a temptation to disobedience were presented, and such an evil made possible.

B.—But could not God, with whom we are told "all things are possible," have interfered in season to prevent the full accomplishment of Satan's designs?

A.—You say "all things are possible" with God. I trust you remember that it is all possible things that are possible with him. "It is impossible for God to lie."—Heb. vi, 18. "He cannot deny himself."—II Tim. ii, 13. He cannot do wrong. He cannot choose any but the wisest and best plan for introducing his creatures into life; and we should bear in mind that the fact of God's not interfering with the introduction and development of sin is one of the very strongest of reasons for believing that evil is necessary and designed ultimately to work good.

C.—Brother A., may I interrupt you here to ask, why, if it was proper and wise that Adam should have a trial under the most favorable circumstances, as a perfect man, should not all his posterity have a similarly favorable trial? We all know that we are born with both mental and physical ailments and imperfections. Why did not God give us all as good a chance as Adam?

A.—If you or I had been in Adam's place, we would have done just as he did. Remember, he had known God only a little while. He found himself alive—perhaps God told him he was his Creator, had a right to command his obedience, and to threaten and inflict punishment for disobedience. But what did Adam know about the matter? Here was another creature at his side who contradicted God, telling him that he would not die from eating the fruit; that God was jealous, because eating of this fruit would make him a God also. Then the tempter exemplified his teaching by eating of it himself, and man saw that he was the wisest of creatures. Can you wonder that they ate? No; as a reasoning being he could scarcely have done otherwise.

C.—But he should have remembered the penalty—what a terrible price he must pay for his disobedience—the wretchedness and death which would follow. If I were so placed, I think I should make more effort to withstand the tempter.

A.—Wait, Brother C.; you forget that Adam, up to this time, was totally unacquainted with wretchedness and death. He could not know what wretchedness meant; he never had been wretched. He did not know what dying meant; and, if you or I had been there, controlled by an unbiased judgment, we would have done just as Adam did. The reason you think you could withstand better is, that you have had experience with evil, and have learned, in a measure, what Adam up to that time had not learned in the smallest degree,—viz., to know good from evil.

C.—O, I see. Then it is because we would have done just as Adam did; that God is justified in counting us all sinners, that "by *one* man's disobedience the many were made sinners," and by the offence of one, all were condemned" (Rom. v, 18, 19), and so "the wages of sin (death) passed upon all," and through or "in Adam *all* die."

B.—Do I understand you to say that God does evil that good may come?

A.—By no means. God did no evil, and he permitted it only because it was necessary that his creatures should *know* good from evil; that by being made acquainted with sin and its consequences—sickness, misery, and death—they might learn "the exceeding sinfulness of sin," and having *tasted* that the bitter "wages of sin is death," they might be prepared to choose life and to understand the wisdom and love of God in commanding obedience to his righteous laws.

B.—But did not God implant in his creature that very thirst for knowledge which led him to an act of disobedience in order to gratify it? Does it not seem, too, that he wanted him to become acquainted with evil, and, if so, why should he attach a penalty to the sinful act, knowing that a knowledge of evil could be obtained in no other way?

A.—We can see readily that a knowledge of evil could be

obtained in no way except by its introduction; and, remember, Adam could not have disobeyed if God had given no commandment, and every command must have a penalty attached to give it force. Therefore, I claim that God not only *foresaw* man's fall into sin but *designed* it: it was a part of his plan. God permitted, nay, designed man's fall; and why? Because, having the remedy provided for his release from its consequences, he saw that the result would be to lead man to a knowledge, through experience, which would enable him to see the bitterness and blackness of sin—"the exceeding sinfulness of sin," and the matchless brilliancy of virtue in contrast with it; thus teaching him the more to love and honor his Creator, who is the fountain and source of all goodness, and to forever shun that which brought so much woe and misery. So the final result is greater love for God, and greater hatred of all that is opposed to him. The best armament against temptation is knowledge.

C.—Your reasoning is clear, forcible, and, would seem to me, plausible, were it not that this experience and knowledge came too late to benefit the human family. Adam failed from want of knowledge and experience to maintain uprightness of character—his posterity, though possessing that knowledge and experience, fail to attain uprightness from lack of ability occasioned by his sin.

B.—I can see no objection to your view, that evil was permitted because necessary to man's development and designed for his ultimate good, were it not as Brother C. suggests—mankind will never have an opportunity to make use of the experience and knowledge thus obtained. But, Brother A., what did you mean a few minutes since when you said God had a remedy provided for man's release from the effects of the fall before he fell?

A.—God foresaw that having given man freedom of choice, he would, through lack of knowledge, accept evil when disguised as an "angel of light;" and, also, that becoming acquainted with it, he would still choose it, because that acquaintance would so impair his moral nature that evil would become more agreeable to him and more to be desired than good. Thus permitted to take his own course, man brought upon himself misery and death, from which he could never recover himself. Then the voice of infinite love is heard: "Behold the Lamb of God that taketh *away* the sin of the world." This is Christ Jesus, and the death of Christ for man's sin was a part of God's plan as much as man's fall. He is "the Lamb slain from the foundation of the world." His death for our sins was purposed by God before man fell; yes, before man was created.

B.—I begin to see a harmony and beauty connected with the introduction of evil which I had not suspected. May we not reasonably say that God could not have displayed those qualities of his nature so attractive to us—*mercy* and *pity*—nor could his *great love* have been made so apparent had not the occasion for their exercise been presented by man's necessities?

A.—I am glad that you have suggested this thought. It is true, that though "the Lord is very *pitiful* and of *tender mercy*," yet neither of these would have been seen had there not been a sinner requiring them; and while "God is *love*," and always has been the same, yet it is true that "in this was *manifested* the love of God, and hereby perceive we the love of God, because he (Christ) laid down his life for us." And do you not see that in the arrangement of the whole plan the *wisdom* of God is beautifully shown? Let me say further, that as we proceed, we shall find God's *justice* made to shine because of the introduction of evil. God might have *told* his creatures of these attributes, but never could have *exhibited* them had not sin furnished an occasion for their exhibition.

B.—I am becoming anxious to see the outcome. You have suggested that Christ is the remedy for man's recovery from the effects of the fall, and that it was so arranged and purposed by God before creating the race, but you have not shown *how* the recovery is effected.

A.—I am glad that you have not lost sight of the real object of our conversation. The answer to this question will involve the consideration of two points:—*First*, What was the penalty pronounced and inflicted? and, *Second*, What was the remedy, and how applied? May I ask you to state in Scripture language what penalty God pronounced on Adam's sin?

B.—I believe it reads, "In the day thou eatest thereof, thou shalt surely die." But he did not die for nine hundred and thirty years.

A.—You quote correctly. The marginal reading will help you over the difficulty of his living nine hundred and thirty years. It is a more literal rendering of the Hebrew text: "In the day thou eatest thereof, dying thou shalt die,"—*i.e.*, from the moment he should disobey God, death would have dominion over him—would have a claim and right to him, and would *begin* its work. It was only a question of time how soon it should lay him low. Elements of disease infested all nature with which he came in contact, since separated from Eden and its trees of life.

We all are in a dying condition, partially dead; mentally, morally, and physically. From the moment of birth, and before it, we have been in the clutches of death, and he never lets go until he has conquered. Man, by means of medical aid, attempts resistance; but, at best, it is but a very brief struggle. Adam, because physically perfect, could offer great resistance. Death did not completely conquer him for nine hundred and thirty years, while the race at the present time, through the accumulated ills handed down through generations past, yields to his power on an average in about thirty-two years.

C.—We are, then, so to speak, overshadowed by death from the cradle to the tomb, the shade increasing each moment until it is blackness complete.

A.—Yes; you get the thought. As David expresses it in the twenty-third Psalm: "I walk through the valley of the shadow of death." The further we go down into this valley the darker it becomes, until the last spark of life expires.

B.—I understand you to believe that diseases of the various kinds are but the mouths of death by which we are devoured, since we were placed within his reach by Adam's sin?

A.—Yes; every pain and ache we feel is evidence not that death *will* get hold of us, but that he *now has* us in his grasp. Adam and all his race have been *in death* ever since he disobeyed.

C.—We frequently speak of death as the "Angel God has sent," "the gate to endless joy," etc., and yet I confess I could never regard it except as an enemy, and such it would really seem to be.

A.—Nowhere in Scripture is it represented as our friend, but always as an enemy of man, and consequently the enemy of God, who loves man; and we are told that "for this purpose Christ was manifest, that he might *destroy death* and him that hath the power of death,—that is, the *devil.*"

B.—If death is the penalty for sin, has not mankind paid that penalty in full when dead? Might he not be released from death the moment after dying, yet fully meet the demand of justice?

A.—"The wages of sin is death,"—not dying, but *"death"* —forever. As well say that a man condemned to imprisonment for life, had received the full penalty in the act of going into prison, as that man received his penalty in the *act of going* into death. By disobedience man fell into the hands of Justice, and, though God is merciful and loving, there can be no warfare between his attributes. Mercy and love must be exercised in harmony with justice. "God is just," and "will by no means clear the guilty." Man was guilty, and must therefore be dealt with by justice. Justice cries, Your life is forfeited, "dying thou shalt die." Man is cast into the great prison-house of death, and Justice, while locking him in, says: "Thou shalt by no means come out thence until thou hast paid the uttermost farthing."

B.—Do I express the same idea by saying that man forfeited his right to life by his disobedience, and, consequently, God, in justice, recognizing and enforcing his own law, could not permit him to live again unless he could meet the claims of justice?

A.—The idea is the same. Man is the debtor, and unless he can pay the debt he cannot come out of the prison-house of death—cannot have life. He cannot pay this debt, and consequently cannot release himself. But man's weakness and helplessness gives occasion for the display of God's mercy and love in Christ Jesus, for "When there was no eye to pity, and no arm to save," God devised a way by which he could be both just and merciful; and so, "while we were yet without strength, in due time Christ died for the ungodly."

C.—How *for* them? His death does not prevent men from dying.

A.—It does not prevent their dying, but it does prevent their continuance in the prison-house of death. He came to "open the prison doors and set at liberty the captives." This he does, not by opposing God's justice, but by recognizing it, and paying that which is due. He has a right to set those prisoners free. In his own death—the just for the unjust—he ransomed us, as it is written, "I will ransom (purchase) them from the power of the grave;" "I will redeem them from death;" "for ye were bought with a price, even the precious blood (life) of Christ."

C.—I understand you to mean, that as Jesus came into the world by a special creative act of God, he was free from the curse which rested upon the balance of the race, therefore not liable to death. As the second Adam he was tried, but came off conqueror. "He was obedient even unto death;" but his right to life not having been forfeited, either through Adam's sin or his own, death had no claim upon it. He, therefore, had an *unforfeited life* to offer Justice as a ransom for the *forfeited life* of mankind.

A.—Yes, as he himself said, "My flesh I will give for the life of the world."—John vi, 51. He must have a right to continuance of life, else he could not give it. He did not conquer nor overthrow Justice, but *recognizing* the justice of the law of God in the forfeit of the sinner's life, he purchased it back with his own, and thereby obtained the right to "destroy death,"—the enemy who for a time is used as the servant of Justice.

B.—Then Justice accepted the life of Christ as a substitute for the sinner's life. But it seems unjust to make the innocent suffer for the guilty.

A.—It would be unjust to *make* or *compel* such suffering, but "Christ *gave* himself for us." "He for the *joy* that was set before him endured the cross."

C.—But how could the life of *one* purchase the life of *many?*

A.—By the rule of

SUBSTITUTION.

As Adam was substituted for the race in trial, and through his failure "death passed upon all men," and all were counted sinners, even before birth, so the obedience *of death* in Christ justified all men to a return to life. Paul so expresses it in Rom. v, 18, [Em. Diaglott]: "For as through the *disobedience* of ONE *man*, the *many* were constituted sinners, so also through the *obedience* of the ONE, the *many* will be constituted (reckoned) righteous;" and, "as through one offense, sentence came on all men to condemnation (condemning them to death), so also, through one righteous act, sentence came on all men to justification of life," justifying their living again.

B.—Shall we understand, then, that the resurrection of the dead is optional or compulsory on Justice?

A.—Christ having "tasted death for *every man*," it is certainly compulsory on Justice to release the prisoners held for sin. Christ's sacrifice having been accepted as "the propitiation (settlement) of our sins, and not of ours (believers) only, but also *for the sins* of the WHOLE WORLD," all *must* go free, *because God is just* to forgive us our sins."—I John i, ix.

B.—Does this imply universal, eternal salvation?

A.—No, it implies the saving or salvation of all men from the Adamic death, but as many of them will be liable to the "second death," on account of their own sin, it *cannot* be *eternal salvation*. The second Adam will eventually restore to the race all that it lost by the first Adam's sin.

C.—Was everlasting life one of the things possessed by Adam before he sinned, and which he lost in death; and is it to be restored to mankind through Christ's ransom?

A.—Yes; his continuance of life, if obedient, is implied in the threatening of death if disobedient. Adam, when created perfect, was possessed of a perfect body, and with perfect arrangements for the continuance of the perfect life, in the trees (woods) of life, in the garden. This kind of life would have lasted *forever* had he continued obedient, hence was *ever*lasting life, conditioned only on obedience. This was lost, and is to be restored to all mankind,—viz., perfection of being, or life and perfect provision for its *everlasting* continuance in harmony with God.

C.—Then this salvation cannot be what Paul refers to, saying, "the gift of God is eternal life."

A.—Natural (human) life—*ever*lasting—was originally *a gift* from God, but its restoration is not, strictly speaking, *a new gift;* rather it is an old gift returned. *Life* once possessed was lost, and is to be restored because *purchased—paid for*—by the death of Christ. The restored race, brought back to where they were before the fall, will have the advantage of knowing from actual experience the character and results of *sin*, which plunged our race in ruin. Then, with the knowledge of sin and its miserable results, gained during the present time, they may be considered superior to all temptation and sin, and, therefore, not liable to death. They will enjoy *everlasting life* in the same sense that Adam possessed it before the fall, and that angels now possess it,—viz., the right and means of continuing their life (by eating, etc., Psalm lxxviii, 25), as long as they continue obedient to God's laws. This is not the same, however, as *Immortality*—the *new gift* of God [see "The Narrow Way to Life."—Tract No. 5] which the Scriptures assert to be possessed by God our Father and our Lord Jesus Christ only, and *promised* to those of the Gospel church, who overcome and become his Bride. This *new gift* was never known of before this Gospel age, "Which in other ages was not made known unto the sons of men as it is *now* revealed unto his holy apostles and prophets by the *Spirit.*"—(Eph. iii, 5; see also I Cor. ii, 10, and I Pet. i, 12.) It "is now made manifest by the appearing of our Saviour Jesus Christ, who hath abolished *death* (obtained the right to do so by giving "his life a ransom for all"), and hath brought *Life* and *Immortality* to light through the Gospel."—II Tim. i, 10.

Yes, our Lord made both things possible, the restoration of *Life* to mankind in general, and the attainment of the superlative degree of life—*Immortality*—by those who overcome and become his bride. It is of this great prize set before believers of this Gospel age that Paul speaks, saying: "God having provided some *better thing* for us." (Theirs was good and grand, but the bride's portion is better.)—Heb. xi, 40.

The character and exclusive application of this promise of the divine, incorruptible, immortal principle of life to the "little flock," the "bride," is shown in the following and other Scriptures,—I Tim. vi, 16: God "*only* hath immortality:" a life incorruptible, independent of any support, eternal (the word *eternal* merely expresses duration, nothing more: God is both *eternal* and *immortal.*—I Tim. i, 17.) In John v, 26, Jesus gives his own definition of *immortality*, claiming that the Father *gives* it to him. "As the Father hath *life in himself,* so hath he *given* to the *Son* to have *life in himself.*" He thus became a partaker of the divine (Jehovah's) nature, a son of God—the "*only* begotten" on that highest plane. And it is to partake of this same *gift* of God—"glory, honor, and immortality"—that his Bride is called. According to his promise she is to become "partaker of the divine nature," also—the same high plane of sonship—"joint heir with Jesus." She is to have within her "a well of water (life) springing up" (Jno. iv, 14), while the rest of mankind may come to the fountain to drink.—Rev. vii, 17, and xxii, 17. Paul says of the overcoming church, "This mortal must put on immortality."—I Cor. xv, 53.

Thus we see that the *new gift* is that held out for the bride—immortality—divinity: while that which the world will get will be the *restoration* of the former life. When the world is restored to perfect human life, possessing the knowledge of good and evil, as perfect obedience will be expected of them as was required of Adam.

C.—You seem to think there are no *conditions* to salvation, while the Scriptures mention them frequently.

A.—There are conditions laid down for attaining the high calling to joint-heirship and dominion with Jesus and *immortality*, but none for the recovery of the race from the fall, except the righteousness and acceptableness of the substitute.

C.—If ransomed, why do they remain in death, and others die, *since* Christ has paid the price?

A.—But the price is not yet fully paid. To have a clear understanding of God's plan, we must recognize the distinction which he makes between the world in general and the Church, or called-out ones of the present time. God loves the world, and has made great and rich provisions, as we have seen, for their coming in *his due time*, to a condition of perfection and happiness, but, in the meantime, while they are getting their experience with evil, God calls out "a little flock," to whom he makes "*exceeding great and precious promises*," conditioned on their living separate from the balance of the world—"overcoming the world,"—viz.: that they may become "children of God," "partakers of the divine nature," the "bride," and "joint heirs," with his only begotten Son, Jesus Christ (anointed).

With her Lord, the wife becomes a part of the Christ—the anointed "body." She now fills up the measure of the afflictions of Christ, which are behind.—Col. i, 24. With him, she bears the cross here and when every member of that body is made "a living sacrifice," has crucified the fleshly human nature, then the ATONEMENT *sacrifice* will be finished, and the bride, being complete, will enter with her Lord into the glory which follows, and share with him in the "joy that was set before him," and which he set before her—of blessing all the families of the earth, thus completing the AT-ONE-MENT between God and the redeemed race. And, "as in the first Adam (and Eve—they being counted as one—Gen. v, 2) *all die*, so in Christ (Jesus and his bride made one—Eph. ii, 15) shall all be made alive." I Cor. xv, 22. Jesus, the head, atoned for his body, his bride, and his righteousness is imputed to her. Being thus justified, and considered holy in God's sight, she is permitted to have fellowship with him in his sufferings that she may also share with him in his glory. [See Tract No. 7, Work of Atonement— Tabernacle Types.]

Behold what manner of love the Father hath bestowed upon us (believers), that we should be called the *children of God*, and if children, then heirs; *heirs of God, and joint-heirs* with JESUS CHRIST, our Lord, *if so be that we suffer with him."*— Rom. viii, 17.

B.—It is very clear to my mind, that a false idea of substitution has obtained among Christian people, from a supposition that it represented God as a vindictive, vengeful tyrant, angry because man had sinned; refusing to show mercy until *blood* had been shed, and caring not whether it was the blood of the innocent or the guilty, so long as it was *blood*. I doubt not many Christians have been led to look upon substitution as a God-dishonoring doctrine, even though there are many scriptures which are found difficult to otherwise make use of, as, " He tasted death for every man ;" "My flesh I will give for the life of the world;" "Without the shedding of blood (life) there is no remission of sins;" "Redemption through his blood;" "While we were yet sinners, Christ died for us;" "We were reconciled to God by the death of his son;" and many other texts to the same effect. It was not by his leaving the glory which he had, nor by his keeping the law, nor by his being rejected of the Jews, a man of sorrows and acquainted with grief, nor by his resurrection, nor by work he has since accomplished, but, "*by his* DEATH *that we are reconciled to God*."

I now see him as mankind's substitute, suffering death, the penalty which the *justice* of God had inflicted upon us. I can see "the exceeding sinfulness of sin" in God's sight, the perfection of his justice, and his great wisdom in so arranging it all, that man's extremity was made the occasion for the manifestation of "the great *love* wherewith he loved us" when "he gave his only begotten Son," and "laid upon him the *iniquity* of us *all*," as well as the love of Christ, who gave *himself* for us, that he might *redeem* us from all iniquity, (buy back to us all we had lost by iniquity). I feel to exclaim with Paul, "O! the depth of the riches both of the knowledge and wisdom of God."

C.—Do you understand the Scriptures to teach that all mankind will reach and maintain the perfection of life which Adam lost—which you called "*everlasting life ?*"

A.—It would seem as though such love, when seen, would beget love and obedience; but we are assured there is a second death, and while those who become subject to it, will not compare in numbers with the saved, yet, there will be some, who will not reach perfection, even at the end of the thousand years, who being incorrigible will be cast into the lake of fire (the second death.)

God made provision before our creation for the recovery from the first death, (the present Adamic death,) but, if after experience with evil and a knowledge of good, they do not appreciate good, they will die for their own sin (not Adam's). There is no recovery from the *second* death—Christ will not die for them again. Justice and love can do nothing more for them.

C.—Do you not understand that some are condemned to the *second death* during the Gospel Age?

A.—Yes, in I Jno. v, 16, and in Heb. vi, 4-6, we are informed that some commit this sin now, but from the conditions mentioned, they are evidently *few*. Only those who have been brought to a knowledge of God and his *good* word and have received the Holy Ghost—in a word, *Saints* are the only ones who could commit it—those who have already received all the benefits of ransom from sin, etc., and who know it. If these, being washed, like the sow, willingly go back to the wallowing in the mire of sin, they commit the sin unto death.

I do not mean simply backsliding, but open apostacy and rejection of Jesus' work of ransom and purchase as explained by the Apostle.

And now there is another thought I would like you to notice: Jesus not only ransomed his bride from *death*, but as her head becomes her leader, example, forerunner, and captain of her salvation to the spiritual condition and divine nature. The death and resurrection of our Lord are inseparably joined: the death was necessary as our ransom, to release us from the condemnation of sin, and to justify us before God; the resurrection was necessary that through our Lord's guidance, grace and strength bestowed through the Spirit we might be able to walk in his footsteps as he hath set us an example—" being made conformable to his death."

B.—I see a force, then, in Paul's expression, Rom. v, 10: "*Reconciled* by the *death*—*saved* by the *life*." His death *justified us to human life*, but his example and aid enable us to "become partakers of the *divine nature*" and life immortal.

C.—If justice could not let mankind go free from death, how could Jesus be permitted to live if he became man's substitute? Must not his life be forever forfeited?

A.—It *was forever forfeited*—he never took the same life again. He was quickened (made alive) to a *higher* life by the Father. He was "put to death in the *flesh*, but quickened by the *Spirit*" to a higher plane, a *spiritual body*. As we shall be, he, our leader, was "*sown a natural body, raised a spiritual body*." Had he risen a fleshly being, with fleshly life, we could not go free. It would have been taking back our "ransom"—our "price." As Paul says, " He took upon him the form of a servant (flesh) *for* the suffering of death." He had no need of it further; he left it. "He made his soul (*life*) an offering for sin:" "My flesh I will give for the life of the world."—Jno. vi, 51. It was given forever. "This man, after he had offered *one* sacrifice for sins *forever*, sat down on the right hand of God," Heb. x, 12, having received a higher life.

B.—This change, then, accounts for his acting so strangely after his resurrection—appearing in different forms—as the gardener to Mary, and "afterwards in *another form* to two of them," etc. His appearing in their midst, the doors being shut, and anon vanishing out of their sight. I often thought it peculiar. But did not his fleshly body disappear from the tomb?

A.—Yes; "His flesh saw not corruption." What became of his flesh, I know not any more than I know what became of the various bodies in which he appeared after his resurrection, and of the various fleshly bodies in which angels appeared at various times. "They saw not corruption;" but, remember, it was not the *atoms of matter* which composed the body—(and which are continually changing)—these *atoms* did not sin, and were not cursed nor forfeited by the fall. It was the flesh *life*, and Christ's laying down his flesh *life*, effects the ransom.

C.—Now, another point: Are all our sins, actual as well as imputed, forgiven?

A.—While all are justified from Adam's sin unconditionally, yet, where knowledge of right is possessed, obedience is expected as far as they are able to obey. Failure in this respect is the occasion for their being beaten with *many* or *few stripes* in the age to come; while the "little flock" who now believe into and are baptized into Christ, become members of *his body*, are by their faith justified from *all things* (Acts xiii, 39), will not be beaten with stripes in the world to come. True, they now receive "chastisement whereof all are partakers," but not *as a penalty;* only as the "rod and staff" of Christ, the Shepherd, to guide his sheep.

Thus the sins of the "Church of the First-born" are passed

over, (not imputed), and she is justified, not from *death* only, but "*from all things.*"

This is beautifully pictured in the *law* by the *Passover.* Wherever in that night the *lamb* was eaten, and his blood sprinkled, the first born was *passed over*—spared.—Ex. 12. So, during this night—the Gospel age—Christ, *our* Passover (lamb) is sacrificed, and we "keep the feast."—I Cor. v, 8. We feed on our Lamb with some of the "bitter herbs" of affliction to sharpen our appetite. All such are passed over. This type shows the *special value* of Christ's death to his body, "The Church of the *First-born.*" Thus, "God is the Saviour of all men, *especially* of those that *believe.*"—I Tim. iv, 10.

C.—Does not the race get back, in the second Adam, *spiritual life*?

A.—Certainly not; Adam was not a spiritual but a *human being,* consequently had human life and powers, which were "very good." Believers of this Gospel age only are warranted by the word of God in expecting a change from human to spiritual conditions—spiritual bodies with spiritual powers "like unto the angels," and "like unto Christ's glorious body." This spiritual condition will be ours "in the resurrection." Those who hope to obtain this *new* nature are influenced by those *hopes and promises* during the present life, and endeavor to live in harmony with that *new* nature. These are said to be "*begotten* of the Spirit through the word of truth that they should be (*at birth*—resurrection) a kind of first fruits of his (God's) creatures."—Jas. i, 18; Rev. xiv, 4. Because of this *begetting* we speak of them as already spiritual beings, though really such in embryo only. Those of our race not *begotten* of these promises, etc., will never be spiritual beings, but as we have seen will be *restored* to *human* perfection.

C.—I have heard frequently your views of restitution, and saw some force and considerable beauty in them, but I never before saw how absolutely certain man's restoration to life is. I see now that the same *justice* of God, which could in no case clear the guilty, could not permit man's release from *death* until the price of his ransom had been paid. The very purity of this justice, as well as the love of God in providing the ransom, assures us that the penalty or price being paid, every man *must* ultimately be released from death. And, Brother A., from one of your remarks I get a beautiful thought,—*i. e.*, That the world's redemption from sin and restoration from death, has been awaiting for 6000 years the coming and work of THE CHRIST (head and body). For over 4000 years it awaited the coming and sacrifice of the Head, and for nearly 2000 years it has also been awaiting the completion and sacrifice of the body. When the body is complete, sacrificed and united to the Head, then follows the glorious restoration of the fallen race. Oh, how grand and glorious it seems! How like a God of infinite wisdom and love.

B.—Yes, yes; it lifts a load from my heart, as I think how God's word is its own interpreter, and shows forth his great, loving plans for all our race. And yet, we can scarcely realize its truth, though thus supported by his Word and commended of our judgment. I presume it is because from infancy we have been bound by false ideas.

A.—And how it seems to unfold itself *now*, just at the time most needed, as the offset of the arguments of infidels; to give confidence and strength to God's children, who are being forced out of, and separated from the worldly-minded churches of today. I consider it a strong evidence that the Gospel age is ending, and that, *therefore*, this message of "Restitution," not due *during* the age, is put into our mouths now. Thus, God is gradually revealing himself through his plans, and the more we know of him, the more we will love and honor him.

C.—One other thought I would like to suggest. Paul speaks of being made a spectacle to angels. Can it be that angels are learning the dreadful effects of sin, from seeing man's experience with it, and the love, mercy, justice, and power of God, in rescuing man from it? The thought presented to my mind is, that this terrible fall, with all its bitter consequences, together with this glorious plan of the ages for the restoration of the fallen race, and the introduction of the new creation, of which Jesus is the head, is intended for the instruction and benefit of *all* God's intelligent creatures, as well as for mankind.

A.—A very good thought. We know that angels are intensely interested in watching the unfolding of the plan. We read in Peter i, 12, "Which things the angels desired to look into," and again (Heb. i, 14), "Are they not all ministering spirits sent forth to minister for those who shall be heirs of salvation?" Probably they are learning for the first time the immensity of God's love, and wisdom, and power—the exceeding beauty of holiness, in contrast with sin, and the lesson of the necessity of entire obedience and complete submission to the will of the one great Master and Father of all, as was beautifully exemplified in his dear Son, our Lord Jesus Christ.

C.—What we have seen relative to *evil* in man—how and why it came—when and how it will be eradicated, its usefulness, yea, necessity, as a protection against future sin, etc., seems not only satisfactory, but a grand solution of a question which has long perplexed me and many others of God's children. Now let me ask, can we go further and learn God's plan relative to *Satan*, the tempter?

A.—Our only source of information on the subject is the Bible, and its accounts, while brief, are to the point, and furnish us all requisite information. Scriptures refer to evil spirits as "legion," or a multitude under a head or prince called Satan. They were at one time angels of God. Peter (ii, 4) and Jude (6) speak of them as—"The angels who kept not their first estate" (of purity and sinlessness) whom God "cast down to *Tartarus* and delivered into chains of darkness."

It is a fundamental law of God's universe, governing all his creatures, that "The soul (being) that sinneth, it shall *die*"— that, in a word, God would supply life to no creature that would not live in harmony with his *righteous laws:* and though in conformity to this universal law, all the rebel angels were from the moment of rebellion *doomed* to die, and must ultimately die, yet God, who we are told " makes the wrath of man to praise him and the remainder (of man's wrath) he will restrain, has acted upon the same principle with the rebel angels. He uses them as his agents in the sense that they accomplish (probably unknowingly) a part of his plan, and give mankind the knowledge of *evil* and its bitter results—sickness, pain, and death of mind and body. And because of this work which they are designed to accomplish, God, the Father, "who only hath immortality" (I Tim. vi, 16)—*life in himself*—the fountain of all life continues for centuries to supply life to these, condemned to death.

I presume that the rebel angels thought that they were *immortal* beings, and that while God could *give* life to any creature, he could *not take it away again*, and probably with pride engendered by this thought of their own hold on life and their supposed inherent greatness, they may have meditated and attempted " a usurpation" of God's authority.

B.—We can see the folly of presuming that he who created and gave life, could not by the same power remand any of those beings again to the same elements from which he created them.

A.—Their rebellion was followed not by death, but by an expulsion from God's presence [to "*Tartarus*"—which probably signifies our *earth*]. This we can imagine a source of trial to the sinless angels. If God had said sinners should *die*, and these having sinned did not die, it would *appear* as though God had been misrepresenting his power. He had power to cast them out of his presence, but *apparently* lacked power to destroy them. Here was apparently a *rival* government nearly as strong as God's, and any who loved evil might desert Jehovah's hosts and join those of Satan.

When *man* was created and placed in Eden, a marvel of perfection and beauty, but on a different plane of being from any previous creation, and with *one power* possessed by none other —the power to propagate his own species, can we wonder if

Satan felt disposed to capture this wonderful creation for allies and subjects? This he did attempt, and approached as a friend who was truly interested in them, and desired their welfare, saying—Why not eat of the "tree of knowledge of good and evil," and be very wise? They said that God had charged them not to eat of it, and had cautioned them that if they ate they would die—lose life and return to the dust from whence they were taken. Ah, my dear friends, says Satan, be not deceived; God has told you an untruth; let me assure you, that you *will* "*not* surely die;" you are immortal beings and can no more die than God himself. Let me convince you that God is deceiving you, because the Lord God doth know that you would become as gods, knowing good and evil; therefore, he seeks to prevent your progress and knowledge by this threat of death. Then Satan ate and died not, and this seemed to corroborate his statements and to make God a liar. I doubt not that Satan thought he told the truth when he said *man* had immortality and could not die. His own experience had evidently been such as to lead him to suppose God could not withdraw life when once given. And the fact that Adam, after sinning, was shut out from fellowship and communion with God, but did not *instantly die*, seemed but a corroboration of Satan's own previous experience.

It was not long, however, until *death* made its appearance, and gave evidence that *man* was "mortal" (Job iv, 17), proving the word of God true and Satan's statement false. We can imagine the awe and terror of the rebel angels,as they saw lifeless Abel, and realized that their theories as to the endlessness of life were thus proved *false*. As they began to see the power of God to destroy as well as to create, they realized that the penalty against them as sinners (death) would sometime be fulfilled. That they *now* realize that their end is *destruction*, is evidenced by the words of the legion to Jesus—"We know thee . . . Art thou come to destroy us?"—Luke iv, 34.

Though now convinced of God's power, they are still his enemies, and use their power to oppose God's plan, etc.; and they are permitted to exércise great power, and *seemingly* to triumph over God's plans and people, but it is only for a time, thank God, and their power is limited; so far can they go and no further.

The untruth which deceived in Eden—" Thou shalt not surely die"—has been the teaching of the devil through all generations since. He has taught it to all heathen peoples, and among those who are God's children—Christians—he has succeeded in getting many to believe him instead of God. But since *death* has come, he offsets the logical conclusions by saying that the real being is not dead; that merely the house has died, and that the being himself you cannot see, that he is *immortal*—indestructible. Upon this falsehood he has built up in the minds of Christian people the belief in a place of endless torment for the supposed endless being, which doctrine is a blasphemy on the character of Jehovah and a contradiction of his word, which repeatedly declares that "the wages of sin is *death*" (not life in torment), and "the soul (being) that sinneth, it shall die" (not live in misery).

By these doctrines and teachings Satan causes the statements of God's word to sound like mockery when it declares—"God is *love*"—"God so loved the world," etc. But while Satan may have supposed that he was opposing Jehovah by making the pathway which leads by *Faith* to glory, rugged and steep and hard to climb, yet we can see that God is still making use of *evil* to accomplish his plans; for the " narrow way," and careful walk and great faith are essential elements in the development of the *little flock*, to whom it is the Father's good pleasure to give the kingdom"—" The Christ (anointed) of God."

Every truth of God seems to be opposed with a specious error, and every error of Satan's which we receive is a hindrance to our reception of some truth of God; and likewise every word of God's truth which we get a firm hold of, repels at once the error of the enemy. Let us give the more earnest heed to the word of God " which is able to make us wise unto salvation" (the great salvation promised to the overcomers—the Bride).

Soon Satan's power must wane. When in God's plan evil has served its designed purposes, the Lord will take to himself his great power and reign (Rev. xi, 17), and the rule which Satan now bears over those who do his will, will be overthrown, and a new age ushered in, the law and controlling power of which will be *righteousness*—a great contrast, indeed, with "the present *evil* world" (age). This taking of control is described by Jesus in a parable—Mark iii, 27. And again, in Rev. xx, 2, it is represented in a pen picture as a *binding* of Satan with a strong chain of power for a thousand years. When bound he has not yet met his doom—destruction—but will merely be restrained from deceiving the nations until the end of the millennial age. Then all mankind having come to *know good and evil*, and having been restored to perfection of being, should and could resist all temptation, and if Satan were again to present temptation, they should oppose it and him, else they are as guilty as he. And so we read, Satan is again permitted to try the restored perfect human family, who now know by experience what sin is, and what God's love is; and, strange as it may seem, a number follow and join the rebellion of the angels—yet we cannot doubt that the number will be *small* in comparison with the numbers who shall *live* in harmony with God.

The agency of evil being then ended, all evil will be wiped out; and "*every* knee shall bow, and *every* tongue confess (Jesus) to the glory of God the Father."—Phil. ii, 11. As Paul declares (writing of Christ and his body-church): "The very God of peace shall bruise Satan (crush the serpent's head—destroy him) under your feet shortly."—Rom. xvi, 20. Paul again declares that the destruction of Satan and the evil which he has caused, was the object of Jesus' coming into the world and dying—" That through death he might *destroy* him that had the power of death,—that is, the *devil*."—Heb. ii, 14.

John also adds his testimony that " For this purpose the Son of God was manifested, that he might destroy the *works* of the devil"—*all evil* (I Jno. iii, 8).

C.—How wonderful it seems! To think that God has for over six thousand years permitted not only men, but angels, to misunderstand his great *wisdom, power, and love* that in due time those attributes might shine with ten-fold brilliancy. This furnishes us a key, too, to our Christian experience. How often, while endeavoring to walk in Jesus' footsteps, and to overcome evil with *good*, we are misunderstood and our purposes maligned. "The world knoweth us not because it knew him not."—I Jno. iii, 1.

B.—I want to say to you before leaving, that I am much rejoiced to see clearly as I now do, why God permitted evil; that it was not, that he had elected ninety to hell to each one chosen for glory, and introduced *evil* as a pretext to justify their damnation: nor, on the other hand, was it because God could not help its introduction, and lacked *wisdom* to foresee, and *power* to avert it; but that he *arranged for its introduction*, and our recovery from it as the embodiment of WISDOM, LOVE, and MERCY.

A.—What a privilege is ours, dear friends, to be living during the fulfillment of the "Seventh Trumpet," during which "the *mystery of God* shall be finished."—Rev. x, 7. As the mystery and cloud of error and evil begins to roll away, and we get a glimpse of our Father's loving plans, how it rejoices and refreshes our hearts to see him as, indeed, a God of Love. Let us lift up our hearts and rejoice, as we see that the glorious Millennial day is dawning, and that soon—

> "His truth shall break through every cloud
> That vails and darkens his designs."

In the light of the unfolding plan, Cowper's lines seem almost an inspiration:

"God moves in a mysterious way,
His wonders to perform;
He plants his footsteps in the sea,
And rides upon the storm.

Deep in unfathomable mines
Of never-failing skill,
He treasures up his bright designs,
And works his sovereign will.

Ye fearful saints, fresh courage take;
The clouds ye so much dread
Are big with mercy, and shall break
In blessings on your head.

Judge not the Lord by feeble sense,
But trust him for his grace;
Behind a frowning providence
He hides a smiling face.

His purposes will ripen fast,
Unfolding every hour;
The bud may have a bitter taste,
But sweet will be the flower.

Blind unbelief is sure to err,
And scan his *word* in vain;
God is his own interpreter,
And he will make it plain."

May we not with angels sing "Glory to God in the highest, on earth peace, good will toward men:"

"Tell the whole word these blessed tidings,
Speak of the time of rest that nears;
Tell the oppressed of ev'ry nation,
Jubilee lasts a thousand years.

What if the clouds do for a moment
Hide the blue sky where morn appears:
Soon the glad sun of promise given,
Rises to shine a thousand years.

A thousand years earth's coming glory—
'Tis the glad day so long foretold:
'Tis the bright morn of Zion's glory,
Prophets foresaw in times of old."

PART II.

WHY WILL THERE BE A SECOND ADVENT?

THAT our Lord intended us as his disciples, to understand, that for some purpose, in some manner, and at some time, he would come again, is, we presume, admitted and believed by all familiar with the Scriptures.

When he said, "If I go away, I will come again," we believe that he certainly referred to his *second personal coming*. Some think he referred to the descent of the Holy Spirit at Pentecost; others, to the destruction of Jerusalem, etc.; but all apparently forget the fact that in the last book of the Bible, written more than *sixty years after Pentecost*, and *twenty-six years after Jerusalem's destruction*, he that was dead, and is alive, speaks of the event as *yet future*, saying: "Behold, I come quickly, and my reward is with me." And the inspired John replies: "Even so *come* Lord Jesus."

Quite a number think that when any are converted, that forms a part of the coming of Christ, and that so he continues *coming* until all the world is converted. Then, say they, he will have *fully* come.

These evidently overlook the fact that the world will not be converted *when* he comes; that the Bible, our only guide on the subject, declares that, "In the *last days* perilous times shall come, for men shall be lovers of pleasure, more than lovers of

God;" that "evil men and seducers shall wax worse and worse, deceiving and being deceived;" and that Jesus gave special warning to his little flock, saying: "Take heed to *yourselves*, lest *that day* come upon *you* unawares, for as a *snare* shall it come upon all *them*" (not taking heed) "that dwell upon the face of the whole earth, and they shall not escape."

Again, we may rest assured that when Jesus said "All the tribes of the earth shall mourn and wail because of him when they see him coming," he did not refer to the conversion of sinners—Do the tribes mourn and wail because of the conversion of a sinner? And if it refers, as almost all admit, to Christ's personal presence on earth, it teaches that *all* on earth will not love his appearing, as they certainly would do if all were converted.

These expect that through the efforts of the Church, the world will be converted, and thus the millennial age be introduced, at the close of which the Lord will come, wind up earthly affairs, reward believers and condemn sinners; that to *convert the world, bind Satan*, make "the knowledge of the Lord to fill the whole earth," and "nations to learn war no more," are the work of the Church in her present mortal condition. When she has accomplished this great and difficult task, Jesus comes to wind it up, etc.

They have much Scripture, which taken disconnectedly, seems to favor this view. But even this, we believe, when God's word and plan are looked at as a whole, will be found to favor the other view,—viz., that Christ comes to reign before the conversion of the world; that the Church is now being tried, and that the reward promised the overcomers is, that they shall share in that reign: "To him that overcometh, will I give to sit with me in my throne."—Rev. iii, 21. "And they lived and reigned with Christ a thousand years."—Rev. xx, 4.

There are two texts in particular used by our post-millennial brethren, to which we would refer:—" This Gospel must first be preached in all the world for a witness. Then shall the end come." They claim this to refer to the Gospel's converting the world before the end of the Gospel age. We pre-millennial believers claim, that *witnessing* to the world does not mean converting the world, but as it reads, to witness or testify.

This witness has already been given. In 1861 the reports of the Bible societies showed that the Gospel had been published in every language of earth; not that all earth's myriads had received it. No; not one in a hundred of the thirteen hundred millions have ever heard the name of Jesus. Yet the text is fulfilled: the Gospel has been preached to every *nation*.

We understand that the main and first object of the Gospel in the present age is, " To take out a *people*, for his name"—the Church—who at Christ's coming are united to him, and receive his name.—Rev. iii, 12.

The second text is: " Sit thou on my right hand, until I make thine enemies thy footstool."—Matt. xxii, 44. The thought generally gathered from this Scripture is, that in heaven God has a throne on which he sits continually, and that when " Christ sat down on the right hand of the Majesty on high," he sat down also upon the same throne. This is a misconception. The throne of God referred to is not a material one, but refers to his *supreme authority* and rulership, for " heaven is my throne and earth is my footstool," and Paul says, " God hath highly exalted him [Jesus] and given him a name above every name." He hath given him *authority* (above every other) next to the Father. If Christ sits upon a material throne until his enemies are made his footstool [all subdued], then, of course, he could not come until the Millennium has been fully inaugurated. But if it means *the exalting to power*, it would not interfere with his coming and subduing all things unto himself.

To illustrate: King William is on the throne of Germany, we say, yet we do not refer to the royal bench, and as a matter of fact, he seldom occupies it. We mean that he rules Germany.

Right hand signifies the chief place, position of excellence or power, and the words of Jesus to Pilate agree with this thought:

"Hereafter ye shall see the Son of Man sitting on the right hand of power, and coming in the *clouds* (storm clouds of trouble.—Zeph. i, 15) of heaven."—Mark xiv, 62. He will be on the right hand *when coming*, and remain at the right hand during the Millennial age. On both views of the subject able arguments are possible, yet both cannot be true. We purpose, therefore, to take a glance at the general

PLAN OF SALVATION,

to see which view is in harmony with it. In so doing, we shall find the relation and bearing of both the first and the second comings, and know where to locate them.

First, then, Has God a plan? All must agree that he has, although almost all are inclined to think and talk of his dealings as though he were dealing by a rule of chance, and governed entirely by circumstance. No; he that would condemn a man for building a tower without first counting the cost, shall he build and people a universe without counting the cost? No, brethren; "Known unto the Lord are all his ways from the beginning." God has a plan, a purpose, and we know that all his purposes shall be accomplished. But how shall we find that plan? It is revealed to us in his word. "Search the Scriptures." Compare Scripture with Scripture, for

>"God is his own interpreter,
>And he will make it plain."

We are too much inclined to ask—What does my church say?—upon any question, instead of—What saith the Scriptures? Too much disposed to consult men's theological opinions, rather than God's Word. With the thought, then, that "the Scriptures are able to make us wise," that "the testimonies of the Lord are sure, making wise the simple," let us examine.

We have learned in the foregoing chapter *Why evil was permitted*. Its existence is attributed in Scripture to the devil. Evil continues because Satan's power is continued. It will last throughout the present age, because the devil is the prince [ruler] of this world.—Eph. ii, 2. He will continue as its ruler as long as he can, or until he is bound. He cannot be bound until a stronger than he takes the control out of his hands.

God, of course, can control him; and of Jesus it is written, "All power in heaven and in earth is given unto me."

But while Jesus has all power, for wise purposes he has not made use of it, permitting evil to reign and measurably control the world, and permitting the devil to be "prince of this world." —John xiv, 30. But the time is coming when "He shall take to himself his great power, and reign," exalting his Church, giving her "power over the nations," so that, instead of, as now, being "subject to the powers that be," she shall "rule the nations." But when will he thus assume control? When the Gospel Church, "His body" (Greek—Ecclesia), is complete. (Evil now being permitted for the trial and perfecting of the saints.) This completion of the Church is attained under the sounding of the seventh trumpet.—Rev. xi, 15. Here the mystery [church] of God is finished, and "the kingdoms of this world become the kingdoms of our Lord and his anointed" [church]. Now, we inquire, is this transfer of authority

FROM SATAN TO CHRIST

caused by the conversion of the nations to Christ through preaching the Gospel? We answer, No. At this time the nations are not converted (vs. 18), "And the nations were angry, and thy wrath is come." If converted, they would not be thus hostile, neither would God's wrath come upon them. On the contrary, God teaches in many Scriptures that a great time of trouble will come upon the nations. "He cometh with clouds" —indications of storm—trouble. "Come, behold the desolations which the Lord hath made in the earth. He maketh wars to cease unto the ends of the earth." This is the way God tells us he will make wars to cease. The next clause informs us that then he will be exalted among the heathen and in all the earth.—Psa. xlvi, 10. This chastisement of nations will be for their good, and is necessary to them as is the chastisement which God now inflicts upon his children, and it will have a good effect, for we read, When the judgments of the Lord are abroad in the earth, the inhabitants of the world will learn righteousness.—Isa. xxvi, 9. It is in this new dispensation that, with evil restrained—Satan bound—"the knowledge of the Lord shall fill the whole earth as the waters do the sea."—Isa. xi, 9. The conversion of the world, instead of being due now while the devil is the prince of this world, will be, David says, "When the kingdom is the Lord's and he is the Governor among the nations; [then] all the ends of the world shall remember and turn to the Lord, and all nations shall come and worship before him.—Psa. xxii, 27, 28.

During the infancy of the human family—say from Adam to Moses—God treated his creatures like very young children. So far as we know, they had very little knowledge of their Creator's power or character. They had scarcely any revelation, the exception being the few cases where God favored certain persons, as Abraham, Lot, and others, communicating to them by angels, giving to Eve and to Abraham peculiar promises, which they could only vaguely comprehend.

The next age was to the Jewish nation a schooling season, during which God taught them to respect his promises and laws. They were yet minors, under age, therefore were treated as children, but kept under the Law, their schoolmaster.—Gal. iii, 24.

While the Word of God was being written and committed to the Jews for keeping, etc., the remainder of the world seems to have been left in the darkness of heathenism. They bowed down to wood and stone, destitute of truth as they are to-day.

In Scripture the period from Adam to the flood is called "the world [age] that was."—II Pet. iii, 6. From the flood to the second coming of the Lord, "the world that now is," and "the present evil world," vs. 7, and the next grand era is called "the world to come."—Heb. ii, 5.

"The present evil world," Gal. i, 4, contains three

SEPARATE AGES.

The *Patriarchal*, lasting from the flood to the death of Jacob; the *Jewish Age*, lasting from the death of Jacob to the death of Christ, when he gave them up, wept over them, and said: "Your house is left unto you desolate;" the *Gospel Age*, lasting from the resurrection of Christ, when he became "the first born from the dead, and the beginning of the new creation," until the full company of "the Church of the First-born" is complete, at his coming. The time of the sounding of the seventh trumpet, the resurrection and reward of prophets, saints, etc.—Rev. xi, 18.

We know not how many ages may be in "the world to come;" but that there is more than one we are sure, for Paul speaks of "the ages to come."—Eph. ii, 7. The first of these alone is dealt with in Scripture—the Millennial age, during which we live and reign with Christ.—Rev. xx, 4.

Having this outline, let us look more particularly at God's doings and sayings, and, first, it will astonish you, doubtless, until you reflect, when I say, that according to his word, God has not *exhausted* his resources for the world's salvation; that, in short, he is not *now* trying to save the world, nor has he been during past ages. What has he been doing? "Taking out a people—Church—for his name." Don't think this wonderful, as it is only putting in a striking form, what all Calvinists believe, among whom are Baptists, Presbyterians, and others,— viz., That God is now electing, or choosing his Church out of the world. Yes, and all our brethren who believe in free grace must admit, that if all his purposes shall be accomplished, and "God's word shall not return unto him void;" if these Scriptures are true, God did not purpose the conversion of the world during the past six thousand years, else it would be accomplished. Neither did he send his word to convert the world up to the present time, else it *did not* prosper in the thing whereto he sent it.—Isa. lv, 11. These two views have been a dividing point in the churches for centuries,—viz.:

ELECTION and FREE GRACE.

We believe the Scripture to teach both, but that it requires the observance of Heaven's first law—*order*, to rightly divide the word of truth on this subject.

First, we will glance at Election. During the age preceding the deluge, there is no Scriptural account of God's giving mankind any law, nor any but very little light of revelation. One promise shines out; the Seed of the Woman was to bruise the Serpent, and even this required future revelation in order to be comprehended. God had, however, a few patriarchs or servants, who had light above the masses as lamp-posts in a dark way.

The Patriarchal age had increase of light. It is now revealed that this seed is not only to crush evil [the serpent], but to "bless all the families of the earth;" still God's Church is represented by single individuals only, Noah, Abraham, Isaac, etc.

These patriarchs were elected—chosen. "God called Abraham and said," etc. Not his kin, but Abraham alone was chosen; he had many sons and daughters, but only Isaac was chosen. "In Isaac shall thy seed be called." Of Isaac's two sons only one was chosen, "as it is written," Rom. ix, 11, 13, "Jacob have I loved, but Esau have I hated," (loved less). God chose before they were born, "that the purpose of God according to election might stand." Now, remember, I do not say that God elected one to go to heaven and the other to go to hell: no, far from it. That is the common misconception of the *Scriptural*, and when properly understood, *beautiful doctrine* of Election.

At Jacob's death another advance step in God's plan is taken, and typical or fleshly Israel is formed. From this time one man no longer represents God in the world; but a nation all the sons of Jacob and their posterity. And now we have an elect na on or church, **and God gives all his special blessings to it.** Other and larger nations—Egypt, Chaldea, etc., are passed by, left without light and without knowledge, while these are given to Israel. "What advantage then hath the Jew? Much every way, chiefly because to them were committed the oracles (laws and testimonies) of God." This is Paul's statement. God speaking to them, says: "You only have I known of all the families of the earth."—Amos iii, 2. This people alone was recognized and thus continued until Christ came. Yes, and after it, for during his ministry he preached to them, and would not suffer his disciples to do otherwise, saying as he sends them out, "Go not into the way of the Gentiles, and into any city of the Samaritans enter ye not." Why so, Lord? "I am not sent but to the lost sheep of the house of Israel."—Matt. xv, 24. All his time was devoted to them until death, and here was his first work for the world—the first display of his free and all abounding grace—

GOD'S GRANDEST GIFT,

not for Israel only, but for all, for "Jesus Christ, by the grace of God, tasted death for *every* man." And now, also, in the Gospel age, a certain sort of election obtains. Some parts of the world are more favored with the Gospel (which is free to all who hear) than others. Contrast yourself, with your privileges and knowledge, with the heathen man who never heard the call. When this called-out company (called to be "sons of God," "heirs of God, and joint-heirs with Jesus Christ, our Lord") is complete, then the plan of God for the *world's* salvation is only beginning. Not until then will "THE SEED" "bruise the serpent's head," and "bless all the families of the earth." For the seed is not Christ, the head, alone, but the Church, which is his body, as Paul informs us, Gal. iii, 16, 29, "Which seed is Christ . . . and if ye be Christ's, then are *ye* Abraham's seed, and heirs, according to the promise." The same company are to bruise the serpent.—Rom. xvi, 20: " The very God of Peace shall bruise Satan under *your feet* shortly."

THE GOSPEL AGE.

The Gospel age makes ready the chaste virgin (church) for the coming Bridegroom. When ready, the Bridegroom comes, and they that are ready are united to him. The second Adam and the second Eve become one, and then the glorious work of restoring mankind begins—" the time of restitution of all things which God hath spoken."—Acts iii, 21. In the next dispensation, new heavens and new earth, she is no longer the espoused Virgin, but the Bride. THEN " the Spirit and the Bride say come, and whosoever will, let him come and drink of the water of life freely."—Rev. xxii, 17.

As Adam, the beginning of the fleshly race, was composed of man, and the helpmeet taken from his side, as it is written, " Male and female created he them, and he called *their* name ADAM."—Gen. v, 2 ; so the "*Second Adam*," of whom Paul says the first "*was a figure*," or type (Rom. v, 14), has a helpmeet taken from his side (redeemed by his blood), and when she is fully formed and perfected, the Bridegroom comes, and they go in to the marriage ; they become *one*, "the new creation of God"—(Read Eph. v, 25, 30, 32), making *in* "*Himself* of twain (Jews and Gentiles) one new man." The Church is composed of both.—Eph. ii, 15. This new man we have found to be the seed " to crush the serpent's head,"—" the seed of Abraham," " in whom all the families of the earth shall be blessed." The Gospel age, so far from closing the Church's mission, was only a school of affliction to enable her, as well as her head to be touched with a feeling of earth's infirmities, that she also might sympathize with mankind, and during the Millennial age assist them, when " the knowledge of the Lord shall fill the whole earth," scattering the darkness of sin and ignorance, causing " wars to cease unto the ends of the earth." These are the " times of restitution," which Peter says are due when Christ comes.—Acts iii, 17, 19. For this " the whole creation groaneth and travaileth in pain together until now, waiting for the *mani-*

festation of the *sons* of God."—Rom. viii, 22, 19. These sons are not now *manifest*. There are among Christ's flock many "wolves in sheep's clothing." Among the wheat there are many tares; but when in "the harvest" ("the end of the age"), they are separated, *then* shall the righteous *shine forth* (be manifested) as the sun in the kingdom of their Father—and *then* to the groaning creation (mankind) shall this "Sun of Righteousness arise, with healing in his wings."

But let us leave this bright and pleasant picture of the coming day, of which with the poet we could say:

"Haste thee along, ages of glory,
Haste the glad time when Christ appears,"

and turning, look at a dark picture. Have you ever asked yourself, while rejoicing in the glorious opportunities to be offered to mankind during the Millennial age,

WHAT ABOUT THOSE WHO HAVE DIED

before the plan of God has thus reached its fullness? There have lived on earth since creation (six thousand years), about one hundred and forty-three billions of human beings. Of these the very broadest estimate that could be made with reason would be, that less than one billion were *Saints of God*—the Church—the Bride. What of the one hundred and forty-two billions who died out of Christ? What is their condition?

Atheism answers: They are eternally dead. There is no hereafter. They will never live again.

Calvinism answers: They were not elected to be saved. God foreordained and predestined them to be lost—to go to hell—and they are there now, writhing in agony, where they will ever remain without hope.

Arminianism answers: We believe that God excuses them on account of ignorance, and that if they did the best they knew how, they will be as sure of being a part of the "Church of the First-born" as is Paul himself.

To this last view the great majority of Christians of all denominations hold, from a feeling that any other view would be irreconcilable with justice on God's part.

But, we inquire, what do the *Scriptures* teach on this last point? That ignorance is a ground of salvation? No; the only condition known in Scripture is FAITH. "By grace are ye saved *through* FAITH." Justification by faith is the ground-rock of the whole system of Christianity. When, on the day of Pentecost, Peter was asked—"What must we do to be saved?" —he answered, "Believe on the Lord Jesus Christ, and be baptized, and thou shalt be saved."

Again he says, Acts iv, 12, "There is *none other name* under heaven given among men whereby we must be saved," than the name of Jesus.

Paul reasons that a man must *hear the Gospel* before he can believe: "How shall they believe on him of whom they have not heard?" This—God's plan—that men shall be saved on account of faith, Paul says was to the Jews a stumbling-block (because they expected salvation as a reward of keeping the Law) and to the Greeks (the worldly-wise) foolishness. But, nevertheless, it has "pleased God, by the foolishness (in the eyes of men) of *preaching* to save

THEM WHICH BELIEVE."

I want to Scripturally close you in to the thought, that all who have not heard could not believe, and not believing, could not be a part of the Bride of Christ. But you object: Paul, in the first two chapters of Romans, teaches, "that these having not the law, are a law unto themselves," and that this law, which their conscience furnishes, is sufficient to *justify* them. No, I answer; you understand Paul differently from what he intended. Paul's argument everywhere is that "all the world is guilty before God." "For if I had not known the law I had not known sin." "For by the law is the knowledge of sin." The law given to the Jew revealed his weakness, and was intended to *show him* that he was *unable* to justify himself before God. "For by the deeds of the Law shall no flesh be justified in his (God's) sight." As the law thus *condemned the Jews*, so Paul says it is with the Gentiles also. Though ignorant of *the Law*, they had light enough of conscience to *condemn them*. (All the light the Gentile could have would not justify sin; it would all the more condemn them, as the written law did the Jew.) "That every mouth may be stopped and all the world may become guilty before God," Rom. iii, 19, in order that eternal life may be seen to be "the *gift* of God, through Jesus Christ, our Lord," to every one that *believeth*.

Well, you answer, the Bible to the contrary, I believe and insist that God won't damn the world for ignorance. Now, let us see. Do you practice what you declare? Why do you assist in sending missionaries to the heathen, at a cost of thousands of valuable lives and millions of money? If they will all be saved, or even half of them, through ignorance, you do them a positive injury in sending them a preacher to tell them of Christ, for we know that only about one in a thousand *believes* when the missionaries do go to them. If your idea be correct, it were far better that no missionary should ever be sent. Before, nearly all saved; now, because of knowledge, nearly all lost. In the same way we might reason that if God had left *all* in ignorance, we would *all have been saved*. Then instead of the Gospel being *good news*, it would be more properly named *bad news*.

No, my brethren; *you do believe* that "there is no other name given whereby we must be saved." Your actions speak the loudest and speak rightly.

Now, suppose we look at these things just as God tells us of them, and leave the clearing of his character to himself.

WHAT HAS BECOME OF THE ONE HUNDRED AND FORTY-TWO BILLIONS?

First, we answer, that you may be sure they are not *now* suffering in hell, because not only do the Scriptures teach that full and *complete* reward is not given to the Church until Christ comes, "when he shall reward every man," but the *unjust* are to receive their punishment *then* also. Whatever may be their present condition, it cannot be their *full reward*, for Peter says: "God knoweth how to *reserve* the unjust *unto the day* of judgment to be punished," and he will do so. But the thought of so many of our fellow creatures at *any* time being lost, without having had the knowledge which is necessary to salvation, seems terrible, indeed, to all who have a spark of love or pity. Then, too, there are a number of Scriptures which it seems difficult to harmonize with all this. Let us see in the light of his dealings how we shall understand the statement, "God is love," or, "God so loved *the world* that he gave his only begotten Son that whosoever believeth in him might not perish."

Ah, Lord, it seems to poor, frail humanity that if you loved the world so much, you might have made provision, not only that believers might be saved, but also that *all might hear*.

Again we read: "This is the true light that *lighteth every man* that cometh into the world." Lord, all our reasons seems to say, not so. We cannot see how Jesus lighted more than a few of earth's billions. Yonder Hottentot gives no evidence of having been so enlightened, neither did the Sodomites and myriads of others.

Once more we read: "Jesus Christ, by the grace of God, tasted death for every man." How, Lord, we ask? If he tasted death for the one hundred and forty-three billions, and from other causes it becomes efficacious only to one billion, is not his death comparatively a failure?

Again: "Behold I bring you glad tidings of great joy, which shall be to *all people*." Surely it is to but a little flock that it has been glad tidings, and not to *all people*.

Another is: "There is one God, and one Mediator between God and man—the man Christ Jesus, who gave himself a ransom for all." A ransom! Then why should not *all* have *some benefit* from Christ's death?

Oh, how dark, how inconsistent do these statements appear when we remember that the Gospel Church is "a little flock." Oh, how we wish it would please God to open our eyes that we might understand the Scriptures, for we feel sure that did we but understand, it must all seem clear; it must all declare in sweetest harmony, *"God is Love."* Oh, that we had the key! Do you want it?—Are you sure you do? It is the last text we quoted: "Who gave himself a ransom for all, *to be testified in due time."* Due time! Ah, now we see! God has a *due time* for everything. He could have testified it to this one hundred and forty-two billions in their lifetime. Then that would have been their due time; as it was not so, their due time must be future. We know that now is our due time, because it is testified to us now. Christ was a ransom for you before you were born, but it was not due time for you to hear it until years after. So with the Hottentot; he has not heard it yet, and may not in this life; but in God's *due time* he will.

But does not death end probation?—one inquires. There is no Scripture which says so, we answer, and all the above and many more Scriptures would be meaningless or worse,

IF DEATH ENDS ALL

to the ignorant masses of the world. The only Scripture ever quoted to prove this generally entertained view, is, "As the tree falleth, so it lies." If this has *any* relation to man's future, it indicates that in whatever condition of knowledge or ignorance he enters death, he remains the same until raised up again.

But can knowledge ever reach these billions in their graves while dead? No; God has provided for the resurrection of them all. For "as in Adam *all* die, even so in Christ shall *all* be made alive." As death came by the first Adam, so life comes by the second Adam. Everything that mankind lost in the first, is to be restored in the second. Hence, the age following Christ's second coming is spoken of as " *the times of restitution."* —Acts iii, 21.

Life is one of the things lost, and is to be one of the things restored. When restored to life with the advantage of experience and knowledge of evil, which Adam had not, he may continue to live *eternally* on the original condition of *obedience*. Perfect obedience will be required, and perfect ability will be given under the righteous reign of the Prince of Peace. Here is the salvation vouchsafed to the world. This enables us to use another text, which is little used except by Universalists, and although not Universalists, yet we claim the right to use all Scripture. It reads: "We trust in the living God, who is the Saviour of *all* men, specially of them which believe." Here are *two classes* of saved ones—*all* (the world) and *believers*. *All* are saved from the Adamic death and *believers* of the present Gospel age receive the special salvation.

When the first-mentioned class (the world) are saved from the weakness, degradation and death to which all are now subject —when they by reason of Christ's ransom are, during the Millennial age restored to human perfection, enlightened by truth and brought to a knowledge of the love of God; if then they will not live in harmony with the law of God's kingdom—Love —they will be "destroyed from among the people."—Acts iii, 23. This is the *second death*.

Now, we see that "the testimony in *due* time," explains all of those difficult texts. In due time it shall be "*glad tidings* of *great joy* to *all* people." In due time, that "True Light shall lighten *every man* that cometh into the world," and in no other way can these Scriptures be used without wresting. We take them to mean just what they say. Paul carries out the line of argument with emphasis in Rom. v, 18, 19. He reasons that as all men were condemned to death and suffered it because of Adam's transgression, so also Christ's righteousness justifies *all* to life again. All lost life, not of their own will or choice, in the first Adam; all receive life at the hands of the second Adam, equally without their will or choice. When thus brought to life, having the love of God testified to them, *their* probation,

THEIR FIRST CHANCE,

begins. We do not preach a *second chance* for any. Since all believers are now "called in one hope of their calling,"—viz.: to be the Bride of Christ, and since this company will be completed at the end of this age, *it* could not be a *second chance* for any in the next age, for there is to be but one *Bride* of Christ.

Peter tells us that the "restitution is spoken of by the mouth of all the holy prophets." They do all teach it. Ezekiel tells us of the valley of dry bones, "This is the whole house of Israel;" and God says to them, "I will bring you up out of your graves and bring you into your own land." To this Paul's words agree, Rom. xi, 25, 26. "Blindness in part is happened to Israel until the fullness of the Gentiles (the elect company 'taken out of the Gentiles,' the Gospel church) be come in, and so all Israel shall be saved," or brought back from their cast-off condition. For "God hath not cast off his people whom he foreknew." They were cut off from his favor while the *bride of Christ* was being selected, but will return to favor when that work is accomplished.—Vs. 28 to 33. The prophets are full of statements of how God will "plant them again, and they shall be no more plucked up." This does not refer to restorations from former captivities in Babylon, Syria, etc., for the Lord says, "*In that day* it shall no more be a proverb among you 'the fathers ate a sour grape, and the children's teeth are set on edge;' but every man shall die for his own sin."—Jer. xxxi, 29, 30. This is not the case now. You do not die for your own sin, but for Adam's—"As *in Adam* all die." He ate the sour grape and our forefathers continued to eat them, entailing further sickness and misery upon us. The day in which "every man shall die *for his own sin*," is this Millennial or Restitution day. But, when restored to the same conditions as Adam, will they not be as liable to sin and fall again as he was? No; they will be liable, but not *as liable;* they will have learned in their present lifetime the lesson which God designs to teach all,—viz., "The exceeding sinfulness of sin." They will then be prepared to appreciate the good and shun the evil, and the Gospel Church then glorified will be, "the kings (rulers) and priests (teachers)" of that new age, for "Unto the angels hath he not put in subjection the world (age) to come, whereof we speak? etc. This restoration to perfect manhood will not be an instantaneous act accomplished in their resurrection, but a gradual work after their resurrection, requiring for its accomplishment all of the Millennial age—"Times of Restitution." And during that time, they shall be rewarded for the "cup of cold water" given (Matt. x, 42) or "beaten with many or few stripes" (Luke xii, 47), according to their improvement or neglect of the measure of light enjoyed during the Gospel age.

There will be something to be gained, and therefore to be sought for by mankind during the next age: Raised to a measure of life, the means of reaching perfection as men will be supplied them, yet they will never reach that condition, unless they put forth effort to obtain it, and make use of the means provided. When made perfect they will have *everlasting life*, in the same sense that Adam had it, and that angels now have it, *i. e.*, on condition of obedience to God's law.

But are we sure that God intends these blessings for any but the "people whom he foreknew"—the Jews? Yes. He mentions other nations also by name, and speaks of their restitution. Let me give you *an illustration that will be forcible.*

THE SODOMITES.

Surely, if we find *their* restitution foretold you will be satisfied. But why should they not have an opportunity to reach perfection? True they were not righteous, but neither were you when God gave you your opportunity. Jesus' own words shall tell us that they are *not as guilty* in his sight as the Jews, who had more knowledge: "Woe unto thee, Capernaum, for if the mighty works which have been done in thee had been done in Sodom, it would have remained unto this day." Thus Jesus teaches us that they had not had their full opportunity. "Remember," Jesus says of the Sodomites, that "God rained down fire and destroyed them all." So if their restoration is spoken of in Scripture it *implies* their resurrection.

Let us look at the prophecy of Ezek. xvi, 48, to the close. Read it carefully. God here speaks of Israel, and compares her with her neighbor Samaria, and also with the *Sodomites*, of whom he says, "I took away as I saw good:" Why did God see good to take away these people without giving them a chance, through the knowledge of "the only name?" Because, it was not their *due time*. They will come to a knowledge of the truth when *restored*. He will save them from death's bondage first, and then give them knowledge as it is written. "God will have *all men to be saved*, and to come to a *knowledge of the truth*."—I Tim. ii, 4. When brought to the knowledge, then, and not until then, are they on trial for *eternal* life. With this thought and with no other, can we understand the dealings of the God of love with those Amalekites and other nations, whom he not only permitted but commanded Israel to butcher. "Slay Amalek utterly—leave neither man, woman nor child." "Spare not the little ones." How often my heart has ached, and yours, too, as we sought to reconcile this apparent wantonness on God's part with the teachings of the new dispensation, "God is love," "Love your enemies," etc. Now we can see, that the entire Jewish age was a type of the higher Gospel age; Israel's victories and conquests merely pictures of the Christian's battles with sin, etc. These Amalekites, and Sodomites and others were used to illustrate, or to be "examples" "for *our* admonition." These people might just as well die so, as of disease and plague, and it mattered little to them, as they were merely learning to know *evil*, that when on trial "*in due time*," they might learn *good*, and be able to discriminate and choose the good and have life.

But let us read the prophecy further. After comparing Israel with Sodom and Samaria, and pronouncing her worse, vs. 53, says: "When I bring again the captivity of Sodom and Samaria then will I bring thy captives in the midst of them." [In death all are captives, and Christ came to "set at liberty the captives and to open the prison doors" of the grave.] In vs. 55 this is called "a return to

THEIR FORMER ESTATE,"

—restitution. But some one who cannot imagine how God really could be so good or just, suggests: God must be speaking ironically to the Jews, and saying he would just as soon bring back the Sodomites as them, but has no notion of either. Let us see. Read vss. 61, 62. Nevertheless, "*I will* remember my covenant with thee; I *will* establish it to the" "Yes," says Paul, "this is God's covenant with them—they are beloved for the fathers' sakes. For the gifts and callings of God are without repentance."—Rom. xi, 27, 29. The sixty-third verse concludes the argument, showing that the promised RESTITUTION is not based on the merits of the Jews, Samaritans or Sodomites— "That thou mayest *remember*, and be confounded, and never open thy mouth any more, because of thy shame, *when I am pacified toward thee*, for all that thou hast done, SAITH THE LORD GOD." When God signs his name to a statement in this way, I must believe it—"*Saith the Lord God.*" And no wonder if they are confounded when in the ages to come he shows forth the exceeding riches of his grace. Yea, many of God's children will be confounded and amazed when they see how "*God so loved* THE WORLD." They will be ready to exclaim with brother Paul: "Oh, the depth of the riches both of the wisdom and knowledge of God! How unsearchable are his judgments, and his ways past finding out."

But some will inquire, How comes it that this has not been seen long ago? We answer, God gives light and knowledge to his people only as it is due. The world was left in almost entire ignorance of God's plan until the *Gospel* age, when Christ came, bringing life and immortality to light through the Gospel. The

Jews up to that time supposed that all the promises of God were to and for them alone, but in *due time* God showed favor to the Gentiles also. Christians generally have supposed that God's blessings are all and only to the Church, but we begin to see that God is better than all our fears; and, though he has given the Church the "exceeding great and precious promises," he has made *some* to the world also.

"The path of the just is as a shining light, that shineth *more* and *more*, unto the perfect day," and the fact that it now shines so brightly, and that we are able to see more of the beauty and harmony of God's word, is strong presumptive evidence that we are in the dawn of that glorious Millennial day, when "we shall know even as we are known."

But we promised to harmonize those doctrines of the Church generally supposed to conflict,—viz., CALVINISM, or *Election*, ARMINIANISM, or *Free Grace*. Perhaps you already see how they harmonize themselves by simply recognizing the order of the ages, and applying each text to the place and time to which it belongs. Let me, then, point out to you

THE INCONSISTENCY OF EITHER CALVINISM OR ARMINIANISM

when separated from each other. In doing so, we do not wish to reflect on those who hold these doctrines. We shall merely call your attention to features which their warmest advocates must confess to be *their weak points*.

First—Calvinism says: God is all-wise; he knew the end from the beginning; and, as all his purposes shall be accomplished, he never could have intended to save any but a few—the true Church—the little flock. These he elected and predestined to be eternally saved; all others were equally predestined and elected to go to hell, for "known unto God are all his works from the beginning of the world."—Acts xv, 18.

This has its good features. It shows, and properly, God's *Omniscience*. This would be our ideal of a GREAT God, were it not that three essential qualities of greatness, viz., MERCY, LOVE and JUSTICE are lacking, for none of these qualities find place in bringing into the world one hundred and forty-two billions of creatures *damned* before they were born, and mocked by protestations of love. No, no. "*God is love;*" "*God is just;*" "*God is merciful.*"

Second—Arminianism says: "Yes, God is love," and in bringing humanity into the world he meant them no harm—only good. But Satan succeeded in tempting Adam. Thus, "sin entered into the world, and death by sin," and ever since, God has been doing all he can to deliver man from his enemy, even to the giving of his Son; and though now, six thousand years after, the Gospel has only reached a very small portion of those creatures, yet we do *hope and trust* that within six thousand years more, through the energy and liberality of the Church, God will have so far remedied the evil introduced by Satan, that all may at least know of his love, and the knowledge of God be co-extensive with the knowledge of evil.

The commendable feature of this view is, that it accepts the statement that "*God is love.*" But, while full of loving and benevolent designs for his creatures, he lacks *ability* and *foreknowledge* adequate to the accomplishment of those loving designs.

While God was busy arranging and devising for the good of his newly-created children, Satan slipped in, and by one stroke upset all God's plans, and in one moment brought sin and evil among men to such an extent that, even by exhausting all his power, God must spend twelve thousand years to even reinstate righteousness to such a degree that the remainder of the race who still live will have an opportunity to choose Good as *readily* as Evil; and the one hundred and forty-two billions of the past six thousand years, and as many more of the next, are *lost to all eternity*, in spite of God's love for them, because Satan interfered with his plans as God had not foreseen. Thus Satan, in spite of God, gets thousands into hell to one God gets to glory.

This view must exalt men's ideas of Satan, and lower their estimation of him who "Spake and it was done; commanded, and it stood fast."

But how refreshing it is for us to turn from these fragments of truth, as separately considered, and

SEE HOW HARMONIOUS

and beautiful they are when united. How, during the present and past ages God is *electing* or gathering, by the preaching of his word, the Gospel Church. How he wisely permitted evil to come into the world, in order that he might develop his church, which, thus "being made perfect through suffering," might be prepared for her glorious work in the future; and how the *masses* of mankind, though not now on probation, are nevertheless getting a knowledge and experience by contact with sin, which he foresaw they would be the better of; and, furthermore, how he took occasion, in connection with this, his plan, to show us his great love, by so arranging that the death of Christ was necessary to our recovery from sin, and then freely giving him, "to be a propitiation for our sins, and not for ours only, but also for the sins of the *whole world*," and then in the next dispensation—

"THE NEW HEAVENS AND EARTH,"

(Rev. xxi, 1–9–10, and xxii, 17)—when "the Spirit and the Bride say come, and whosoever will may come and take of the water of life freely," he will show his "*Free Grace*" in fullest measure.

This period of his presence and reign is commonly known among Christian people as the *Millennium*, which means one thousand, and which is applied to the time future, "when the earth shall be full of the knowledge of the Lord as the waters cover the sea" (Isa. xi, 9), and none need to say unto his neighbor, "Know thou the Lord?" "*All* shall know him," etc. The time when there shall be no more curse (Rev. xxii, 3), "when the desert shall blossom as the rose (Isa. xxxv, 1), and "streams shall break forth in the deserts" (Isa. xxxv, 6), when "the tabernacle of God will be with men and he shall dwell with them" (Rev. xxi, 3), when Satan shall be restrained and righteousness shall control. "Then nation shall not lift up sword against nation," "nor learn war any more;" but "they shall beat their swords into plow-shares, and their spears into pruning-hooks" (Micah iv, 3). Glorious prospect for the world!

>   "Haste thee along, ages of glory,
>   Haste the glad time when Christ appears!"

Is not this the teaching of God's word? Men never would have thought of such a *glorious plan* of salvation. Truly God has said: "My ways are not your ways, nor my thoughts your thoughts." Hereafter when we address him, "Our Father," may it call to our mind that his love and compassion are far greater than the pity of our earthly parents; and while we study his words more and more, and seek to "*grow in grace*, and in the *knowledge* and *love* of God," let us ever remember that—

>   "Blind unbelief is sure to err,
>   And scan his word in vain.
>   God is his own interpreter,
>   And he will make it plain."

Having seen how much of the great plan of God awaits the coming of Christ for its accomplishment, and having, we trust, found *why* Christ comes, can we help loving his appearing?

THE UNPARDONABLE SIN.

"WHOSOEVER speaketh a word against the Son of Man it shall be forgiven him; but whosoever speaketh against the Holy Ghost it shall not be forgiven him, neither in this world, neither in the world to come.—Matt. xii, 32. [The word here rendered world, as in many other places, should be rendered *age*, and is so rendered in all new translations.]

This text teaches first that there is such a thing as *forgiveness of sins* both in the present Gospel age and in the coming—Millennial—age. The basis of all forgiveness of sins, is in the fact that "Christ died for our sins."

Secondly, it teaches that some sins are possible, which God will not reckon as a part of the Adamic sin which passed upon all men and which is to be *forgiven* all men. If men looked at Jesus and ignorantly supposed him an impostor and blasphemed him, it would be excusable and forgivable as a result of the *fallen* nature. Even should they blaspheme the name of God, and say they believed in no such being, etc., this too might be forgiven for the same reasons. But when God's *power* (the Holy Ghost) was *manifested* in doing them good as it was manifested through Jesus, there certainly was no excuse for even the most depraved of men ascribing those good works to an *evil power*—Satan. And this is just what Jesus tells them, that such conduct cannot be classed as a part of the general human depravity, and it therefore cannot be *forgiven*.

The light was shining so clearly, that though their eyes were nearly blinded by sin, they could not help realizing some of the *light* as Jesus manifested some of "the powers of the world (age) to come." As he said to them on another occasion, their "stripes" (punishment) in the next age will be in proportion as they have been *able to comprehend and do* justly and have not so done. They whose moral sight and hearing have been totally destroyed by Adam's sin and its results (if any such there be— the Lord knoweth) will have *no stripes* in the future, will be *forgiven* fully. They who see a little and could obey a little and do not so do, shall be forgiven the things they did not see and could not do, but will be *beaten* (punished) with a few stripes for the few things they saw, and could, but did not do. They who saw more and whose ability to perform was *less* impaired by the fallen nature, and who fail to do according to their ability, are to be beaten with *many stripes*.

Now notice that all who receive "*stripes*" receive them for *unpardoned* sins, for if the sins were *pardoned* they would not be punished for them. In our earthly courts if a man had trespassed against the law in two ways, and the penalty of the first crime was imprisonment for five years, and for the second six months; if it could be shown that he was not really to blame for the first crime, but was forced into it by circumstances over which he had no control, but the second crime was measurably under his control, the decision of the court would be "*guilty*" on both charges: but he would be *pardoned* on the first charge and not on the second; the result would be that he would serve the six months' punishment.

Here are two earthly crimes, one pardonable and one *unpardonable*. So it is with God's law; all are sinners and condemned —guilty—on account of Adam's sin, but the full ransom from that sin has been paid, and so though condemned before the court of heaven, it is announced that all of our imperfections traceable to that cause are freely and fully forgiven. But neither more nor less is pardonable. All sins against *light and ability* are unpardonable, cannot be forgiven at any time, and hence *must be punished*. The world will have many such sins to be punished in the age to come, and they receive in some instances much punishment in the present life and age. In a word, all punishment indicates unpardoned sin, for if it were pardoned it would not be punished as well.

Paul tells us of extreme cases of this sort of *unpardonable* sin. Men of the world who have a *little* light we have seen can commit it, but when a man becomes a Christian and has the eyes of his understanding opened—when he is brought from the condition of darkness and ignorance, into the *light of the knowledge* of the Lord, to then "sin *willfully*" is terrible indeed. Due and full allowance is made for all our weaknesses and imperfections which come to us through our fallen nature, and which clog and hinder our doing as we should wish to do—our Father's will: but no more. If we cease to desire to do God's will, we cut loose from our Lord and begin to walk according to our own will as *natural* and no longer spiritual beings. This is the thing pictured by the proverb: "The dog is returned to his vomit, and the sow that was washed to her wallowing in the mire."—II Pet. ii, 22.

In Heb. vi, 4-6, Paul assures us that any Christian who has reached a full and mature development in the spiritual life, having "been *enlightened*," "tasted of the heavenly gift," "been made partaker of the Holy Ghost," "tasted of the *good* word of God" —if such shall fall away, it is impossible to renew them *again* unto repentance. Why? Because this is an unpardonable sin. But can they not be *punished* for this sin and thus be free from it in time? No, with the above description of the Apostle, we understand that these had enjoyed all the blessings due them on account of Christ's ransom: *i.e.*, they were reckoned of God *justified from all sin*, as *new* creatures had been brought to a condition of enlightenment and knowledge of the Lord's will, and then, had *deliberately and willfully* acted contrary to it. We do not refer to a child of God *stumbling* or being overcome of the old nature for a time, but as expressed in Heb. x, 26—"if *we* sin willfully after that we have *received the knowledge* of the truth, there remaineth no more (a) sacrifice for sins, but a certain fearful looking for of judgment and fiery indignation which shall devour (*destroy*) the adversaries."

In a word, we understand Paul to teach that the class here described have received all the benefits due them through Christ's ransom, and that their willful sinning against knowledge, etc., places them in the same position as Adam occupied when he sinned; the penalty of all such willful sin is *death*. In Adam's case it was the *first* death. In the case of these it is the *second death*. They had been *reckoned dead* as Christians, and then *reckoned of God alive* as new creatures, and now they die for their own willful sin—*the second death*. There is neither forgiveness nor excuse for such sin; they must have the full penalty and die. They have *lightly* esteemed the ransom *after* they knew of it, and thus have "trodden under foot the Son of God and counted the blood of the covenant *wherewith they were sanctified* (set apart as new creatures) an unholy (ordinary—common) thing, and done despite (disrespect) unto the spirit of (favor) grace."

These have no hope; they could not be recovered from the *second* death in any other way than as Adam and his children were redeemed from the *first* death—*i. e.*, by some one *dying* for their sin as Jesus died for Adam's sin. Will Jesus die again for them? No, "Christ being risen dieth no more; death hath no more dominion over him." Nor could there be any object in bringing such to life again; having had full redemption, and having come to know both *Good and Evil*, if they love evil rather than good and *willfully* do it, let them be deprived of life. All will say it is love on the part of our Father to deprive them of life, which, if continued, would be only of injury and evil both to themselves and others.

It will readily be seen that *this sin* to this last mentioned extent—punishable with the *second death*—could not possibly have been committed prior to the Gospel age, since not until Pentecost did the Holy Ghost come as a teacher to guide the church into the truth.—John xvi, 13. It had in past time been active through holy men of old, as they—"spoke and wrote as they were moved by the Holy Ghost," but it moved them to *write* but *not to understand.* It came upon the prophets as *servants* to communicate; it comes to us as a *seal* of *sonship*, and to enable us as sons to *understand* our Father's will.—Rom. viii, 14. Consequently in previous ages none ever "*tasted* of the good word of God," or "became *partakers* of the Holy Ghost," etc., and consequently none who lived in past ages could sin away *forever* all hope of a future life.

The millions of past ages never have been recovered from the *first* death (Adamic) in any sense, and must be so recovered before it will be possible for them to commit the "sin unto *death.*"—Heb. vi, 4, 6. That Israelites, Sodomites, Egyptians, and others have not fully lived up to the knowledge they possessed we doubt not, and they will doubtless, therefore, have "*stripes*" in the coming age for sins not pardoned by Jesus' ransom.

We are glad to say that we believe very few have ever committed this "*Sin unto death;*" that *very few* ever possessed the *knowledge, etc.*, specified by the apostle, we feel sure ; and that is the specified condition.

"There's a wideness in God's mercy,
Like the wideness of the sea ;
There's a kindness in his justice
Which is more than liberty."

PART III.

HOW WILL CHRIST COME?

To ALL who "love his appearing" and have read with interest the foregoing chapter, the manner in which our Lord will come becomes a subject of great interest, and now invites your attention.

At his first advent he came in a body of flesh prepared "for the suffering of death:" at his second advent he comes *in glory* (Mark xiii, 26) *in his glorious body* (Phil. iii, 21), *a spiritual body*.—I Cor. xv, 44-49.

But what is a spiritual body? What powers are theirs, and by what laws are they governed? We are here met by the objections—we have no right to pry into the hidden things of God —and "Eye hath not seen, ear heard, neither have entered into the heart of man the things which God hath prepared for them that love him." To both of these propositions we assent, but believe we cannot find out by studying God's Word what he has not revealed; and our investigation will be confined to the Word. The above quotation of Scripture (I Cor. ii, 9) refers to the natural or carnal man, and by reading it, in connection with the three verses which follow, the objection vanishes; for, says the apostle, "God hath revealed them unto *us* by his spirit," which was given to us believers—the church—"that we *might know* the things that are freely given to us of God." And in the last clause of vs. 13, he gives us the rule by which we may know,—viz., "Comparing spiritual things with spiritual." We are very apt to change this rule, and compare spiritual things with natural, and thus get darkness instead of light. Let us now use the apostle's rule.

There is a spiritual body as well as a natural body; a heavenly, as well as an earthly body; a celestial as well as a terrestrial; a glory of the earthly, as well as of the heavenly. The glory of the earthly, as we have seen, was lost by the first Adam's sin, and is to be restored to the race by Jesus and his bride during the Millennial reign. The glory of the heavenly is as yet unseen, except as revealed to the spiritual, "*new* creatures"—to the eyes of faith, by the Spirit, through the Word. They are distinct and separate.—I Cor. xv, 38-48. We know what the natural, earthly, terrestrial body is, for we now have such; it is flesh, blood, and bones; for, "that which is born of the flesh is flesh," and since there are two kinds of bodies, we know that the spiritual is not composed of flesh, blood, and bones, whatever it may be; it is a heavenly, celestial, spiritual body,—"That which is born of the spirit is spirit." But of what material a spiritual body may be we know not, for "it doth not yet appear *what* we shall be; but . . . . we shall be like him"—Jesus.

THE SECOND BIRTH.

Jesus was raised from the dead a spiritual body; this was his second birth. First born of the flesh a fleshly body—for, "as the children are partakers of flesh and blood, he also himself likewise took part of the same."—Heb. ii, 14. He was "Put to death in the flesh, but quickened [made alive] by the Spirit." He was raised a spiritual body. He was the "first *born* from the dead," "the first-*born* among many brethren." The church are those brethren and will have a second birth of the same kind as his,—*i. e.*, to spiritual bodies by the resurrection, when we shall awake in his likeness—being made "Like unto *Christ's glorious body*." But, this second birth must be preceded by a begetting of the spirit—at conversion—just as surely as a birth of the flesh is preceded by a begetting of the flesh. Begotten of the flesh—born of the flesh—in the likeness of the first Adam, the earthly; begotten of the spirit—in the resurrection born of the spirit, into the likeness of the heavenly. "As we have borne the image of the earthly, *we* shall also bear the image of the heavenly." We may, then, by examining facts recorded of Christ, after his resurrection, and of angels, who are also spiritual bodies, gain general information with regard to *spiritual bodies*, thus "comparing spiritual things with spiritual."

First, then, angels can be, and frequently are, present, yet invisible. "The angel of the Lord encampeth round about them that are his, and delivereth them;" and "Are they not all ministering spirits, sent forth to minister for them who shall be heirs of salvation?"—Heb. i, 14. Are you begotten of the spirit, an heir of salvation? Then doubtless they have ministered to you. Have they ministered visibly or invisibly? Undoubtedly the latter. Elisha was surrounded by a host of Assyrians; his servant was fearful; Elisha prayed to the Lord, and the young man's eyes were opened, and he "saw the mountains round about Elisha full of chariots of fire and horsemen of fire" (or like fire). Again, while to Balaam the angel was invisible, the ass's eyes being opened saw him.

Second, angels can, and have appeared *as* men. The Lord and two angels so appeared to Abraham, who had a supper prepared for them, of which they ate. At first Abraham supposed them to be "three men," and it was not until they were about to go that he discovered one of them to be the Lord, and the other two angels, who afterward went down to Sodom and delivered Lot.—Gen. xviii, 1. An angel appeared to Gideon *as a man*, but afterward made himself known. An angel appeared to Samson's mother and father; they thought him a man until he ascended up to heaven in the flame of the altar.—Judges xiii, 20.

Third, spiritual bodies are glorious in their normal condition, and are frequently spoken of as glorious and bright. The countenance of the angel who rolled away the stone from the sepulchre "was as the lightning." Daniel saw a glorious spiritual body, whose eyes were as lamps of fire, his countenance as the lightning, his arms and feet like in color to polished brass, his voice as the voice of a multitude; before him Daniel fell as a dead man.—Daniel x, 6. John, on the Isle of Patmos, saw Christ's glorious body (Rev. i, 14), and describes the appearance in almost the same language—His voice was as the sound of many waters, his eyes as lamps of fire, his feet like fine brass as it burns in a furnace (so bright that you can scarcely look at it). John falls at his feet as dead; but he said to him, fear not; "I am he that was dead; behold I am alive forevermore." Saul of Tarsus saw Christ's glorious body. It shone above the brightness of the sun at noonday. Saul lost his sight and fell to the ground.

We have thus far found spiritual bodies truly glorious; yet, except by the opening of our eyes to see them, or their appearing *in the flesh as men*, they are invisible. This conclusion is further confirmed when we examine the more minute details connected with these manifestations. The Lord was seen of Saul alone, "they that journeyed with him .... seeing no man."—Acts ix, 7. The men that were with Daniel did not see the glorious being he describes, but a great fear "fell on them, and they ran and hid themselves." Again, this same glorious being declares: (Daniel x, 13) "The prince of Persia withstood me one and twenty days." Daniel, the man greatly beloved of the Lord, falls as dead before this one whom Persia's prince withstands one and twenty days. How is this? Surely, he did not appear in glory to the prince. No; either he was invisibly present with him, or else

HE APPEARED AS A MAN.

Jesus is a spiritual body since his resurrection. He was "raised a spiritual body," consequently the same powers which we find illustrated by angels—spiritual bodies, should be true also of him, and such was the case. If Jesus had revealed himself to his disciples after his resurrection, as the angel did to Daniel, the glory of the spiritual body would undoubtedly have been more than they, as earthly beings, could bear. They would probably have been so alarmed as to be unable to receive instructions. [We understand that the glorifying, spoken of was accomplished after he ascended to the right hand of the Majesty on High (Jno. vii, 39), refers to the installation into the majesty of power. When the Scriptures speak of a glorious spiritual body, the glory, grandeur of *the person* is referred to, and not the glory of power or office.] During the forty days of his presence before ascension, he appeared some seven or eight times to his disciples; where was he the remainder of the time? Present but invisible. Notice, also, that in each instance, he is said to have *appeared*, or he *showed himself*, language never used of him before his change from a natural to a spiritual body; now, as angels do, he *appeared*, etc.

Remember that the object of Jesus' appearing to them was to convince them that "he who was *dead* is *alive* forevermore;" that they might go forth as "*witnesses*." Being a spiritual body, it was simply a question of expediency which way he could best appear to them—*i. e.*, in which way would his object in appearing be best accomplished. He *could* appear as a "flame of fire," as the angel of the Lord had appeared to Moses "in the burning bush." Thus, Jesus *might* have appeared to and talked with the disciples, or he might have appeared in glory as the angel did to Daniel, or as he afterward did to John and to Saul of Tarsus. If he had so appeared, they would doubtless also have had "great fear and quaking," and would have fallen to the ground before him, and "become as dead men;" or he could do as angels had done, and as he had done with Abraham (Gen. xviii) when he appeared *as a man*. This last he saw to be the best way, and he did appear *as a man*. But notice, they did not see him after his resurrection *as* before his death. First he appeared to Mary as the gardener, and she "saw Jesus standing and knew not that it was Jesus." "After that he *appeared in*

ANOTHER FORM unto two of them as they went into the country" (Mark xvi, 12). They knew not that it was Jesus until he revealed himself in breaking of bread; then he *vanished* from their sight. Notice, it was in "*another form*," and, consequently, not the same one in which he appeared to Mary.

Again, some having given up all hope of being any longer fishers of men, had gone again to their nets. They had toiled all night and caught nothing. In the morning Jesus is on the shore within speaking distance, but they "knew not that it was Jesus." It was *another form*. He works a miracle, giving them a boat-full of fish in a moment. John, the loving disciple, remembers the feeding of the three thousand and five thousand, the strange days in which they were living, and that Jesus had appeared to them already. He seems at once to discern who gave the draught of fishes and said: "It is the Lord." He recognized him not by the natural eye, but by the eye of faith, and when they were come to shore "None of them durst ask him, Who art thou? knowing (feeling sure from the miracle, for they saw not the print of the nails) that it was the Lord" (John xxi, 1). Thus did Jesus appear to his disciples at different times, to make of them witnesses of his resurrection. He was present, but unseen, during most of those forty days, appearing, in all, perhaps not more than seven times.—John xx, 26, and xxi, 14.

We presume that it was to guard against the idea that he was a *fleshly body* that he appeared in various *forms* and in miraculous ways, coming into their midst, the doors being shut, and vanishing from their sight. He not only showed that *he* had undergone a change since death, but he illustrated his own teaching to Nicodemus, that every one born of the Spirit ("That born of the Spirit *is Spirit*") can go and come like the wind. "Thou canst not tell whence it cometh and whither it goeth, *so is every one* that is born of the Spirit" (Jno. iii, 8). So did Jesus go and come. "But some doubted"—some wanted to thrust their hands into his side, and put their fingers into the print of the nails; and Jesus thus appeared. Whether it was the same body that had been crucified, or one like it, we know not, nor does it make any difference; in any case, it was not *his body*, for he had been "quickened of the Spirit"—a spiritual body—"sown a natural body, raised a *spiritual body*," and none of the various *forms* or *bodies* in which he appeared were *his body*. They were only *vails of the flesh* which hid or covered the glorious spiritual body, just as angels had often used the human form to vail themselves when appearing to mortals.

One point which seems to confuse is, that Jesus ate and drank with the disciples and said, "Handle me, for a spirit hath not flesh and bones, as ye see me have."

Jesus affirms just what we have claimed, that the body they saw and handled, and which ate with them, was not his spiritual body, for he says: "A spirit *hath not* flesh and bones." Look back to the time when the Lord and two angels appeared to Abraham (Gen. xviii). Jesus had not then left "*the form of God*," and taken the *form of a servant*. He was a spiritual body then, and it had not flesh and bones, but he then used the human form as a vail. He ate and drank and talked, and could have said to Abraham: Handle me; this body which you see is "flesh and bones." No, the disciples did not see Christ's glorious spiritual body, but they saw the fleshly "*forms*" in which he appeared.

St. Paul teaches us (I Cor. xv, 44, 45) distinctly that Christ was raised from the dead a life-giving *Spirit* [*pneuma*, the same word used by our Lord]. But where did he get the various bodies in which he appeared, and where did they go when their work was accomplished? They did not see corruption; neither did those bodies which the angels used see corruption. Our only answer is, "Thou canst not tell whence it cometh nor whither it goeth." But we all believe other things which we cannot fully understand. We cannot understand *how* a grain of wheat grows, yet we know it does grow; we know not *how* Jesus turned the water into wine, or healed the sick, or raised the dead. Yet we believe that he did these things. Can you tell where he got the clothes he wore after his resurrection? "They parted his raiment among them, and for his vesture they cast lots"—the old were gone, and the linen clothes lay in the sepulchre. Is it more difficult for spiritual beings with their powers to create a covering of flesh than a covering of cloth? No; the same power can and did do both.

Thus we have found Jesus' spiritual body and those of angels glorious, yet invisible to mortals: with power to manifest the glory, or to appear as men, or in any form they may choose. In the resurrection the overcomers—the Bride—shall be "like unto Christ's glorious body." "We shall be like him, for (not until then) we shall see him as *he is*" (not as he was, for "though we have known Christ after the *flesh*, yet now, henceforth, know we him, no more" [after the flesh] (II Cor. v, 16). Such a spiritual being was Christ at the time of his ascension; and, with what we have learned of the powers of that spiritual body, we are now, we hope, prepared to inquire:

HOW WILL HE COME AGAIN?

Briefly stated, we believe the Scriptures to teach that our Lord will never again appear as a man; that at his second coming he will be invisible to mankind; that none will ever see him except the Church: "Without *holiness* no man shall see the Lord;" that the Church will not see him until changed from natural to spiritual bodies; that then "we shall see him *as he is*" [not as he was], for "we shall be like him" [not he like us, as at the first advent]. But, while none are to see him with their natural eyes, all are to *recognize* his presence and his power ("the *eyes of their understanding* being opened"). Hence we read: "Every eye shall see (*optomai*—recognize) him."

There will be, we understand, various orders and times of recognizing him by various classes of humanity. The first class to recognize his *presence*, the Bible teaches, will be those Christians who live in most intimate communication with him, and who are the most separate from the world. These, by the eye of faith, through the word of truth, will recognize him as present. These, called "a little flock," the "overcomers," the Bride, etc., will be the first to be informed of his presence. We have a "sure word of prophecy, whereunto ye do well that you take heed, as unto a light that shineth in a dark place, until the day (of the Lord) dawn." "If thou shalt not watch, ... thou shalt not know what hour I will come upon thee." This "little flock" will be changed—made like unto Christ's glorious body.

Then commences a time of trouble on the worldly-minded Church, and on the world, in which the Lord makes known his presence and power, by causing the overthrow of all systems of error, in Church and world.

Though all this uprooting and overturning of governments, etc., will be accomplished in a manner considered perfectly natural, yet it will be so thorough, that ultimately all will realize that "The Lord reigneth," for "he shall be revealed (made known) in flaming fire." (Judgments.) And in due time, "all that are in their graves" shall also be brought to life (during the Millennial age), and recognize Christ; for "Unto him every knee shall bow." Thus every eye shall see him; and *they also which pierced* him."

Now let us examine the subject more in detail.

The second advent, like the first, covers a period of time, and is not the event of a moment. The first lasted nearly thirty-four years, and the events connected with it—his birth, baptism, sorrow, death, resurrection, etc., as mentioned by the prophets, all took place *at* the first advent. The second advent, as we shall see, lasts much longer. It includes the Millennial reign, and prophecy covers all the prominent features of that reign. He comes to reign—must reign until he has put down all enemies; the last being death.—I Cor. xv, 25, 26.

In the application of prophecy to the events of the first advent, we recognize order. Christ must be the "*child* born and son given" "before the *man* of sorrows and acquainted with grief." He must *die* before he could *rise* from the dead, etc. So also in studying prophecy, referring to the second advent, we must recognize order; we must judge of the order somewhat by the character of the event. As the wife is the *glory* of the husband, so the Bride is the glory of Christ, for we are to be "partakers of the glory that shall be revealed (I Pet. v, 1, 10), and as the "glory shall be *revealed in us*" (Rom. viii, 18), we know that Christ could not come in the glory of his kingdom [church] until he has first gathered it from the world. In harmony with this thought we read—When *he* shall *appear, we* "also shall *appear with him* in glory."—Col. iii, 4.

The prophets foretold the sufferings of Christ [head and body] and the glory that should follow.—I Peter i, 11. If the sufferings were of the *whole body*, so is the *glory*. We suffer with him that we may be also "*glorified together.*"—Rom. viii, 17. "Enoch prophesied, saying—the Lord cometh *with* ten thousands of his saints," [gr. *hagios*, never translated angel] (Jude 14). Again (Zach. xiv, 5), we read—" The Lord my God shall come and *all the saints with thee.*" Thus we learn that when he *appears* in glory we are *with* him, and of course, we must be caught to meet him before we could appear *with* him. We understand that this *appearing* of the saints *in glory*, as already expressed of the Lord, will be a manifestation not in person but in *power*.

We have evidence to offer, proving that he comes unknown to the world; but attempt to answer two supposed objections first,—viz.: "This same Jesus shall so come in like manner as ye have seen him go into heaven," (Acts i, 11), and "The Lord himself shall descend from heaven with a shout, with the voice of the Archangel and the trump of God; and the dead in Christ shall rise."—I Thes. iv, 16. These texts are supposed to teach that Christ will come in a manner visible to the natural eye, while the air is rent with the blast of the Archangel's trumpet, at which, mid reeling tombstones and opening graves the dead will be resurrected. It certainly has that appearance on the surface, but look at it again: Would that be coming in *like manner* as they saw him go? He did not go with the sounding of a trumpet and outward demonstration. It does not say, *you shall see* him coming, nor that *any one* would see him, but—he shall come. When he arrives it will be privately. He comes to organize the Church as his kingdom, to set it up. He comes to be glorified in his saints in that day.—II Thes. i, 10. The world saw him not after his resurrection; they did not see him ascend, as he said, "Yet a little while and the world seeth me no more."

And "he shall so come in like manner"—unknown to the world. Nor will they see (recognize) him in his second advent until his Church is gathered, for when he shall *appear* "we also shall *appear* with him." What, then, does the trumpet mean? Let us see. We are to be rewarded "at the resurrection." As we will not be rewarded twice, nor resurrected twice, we conclude that the "Trump of God" (I Thess. iv, 16) and the "Last Trump" (I Cor. xv, 52) are the same, differently expressed.

The same events are mentioned as occurring at each—*i. e.*, the resurrection and reward of saints. And for the same reason we believe the "Trump of God" and "Last Trump" to be the "Seventh Trump" of Rev. xi, 15. The "Seventh Trump" is the "Last Trump," and is called "the Trump of God," possibly because introducing the special judgments of God connected with the setting up of his kingdom.

These trumpets evidently are the same—but what? The seventh angel *sounded*. A sound on the air? No, not any more than the six which preceded it. They are each said to *sound*, and Sir Isaac Newton, Clarke, and all commentators of note, agree that five or six of these trumpets are in the past. They have been fulfilled in *events* upon the earth, each covering a period of time. They certainly must all sound before the resurrection, for that is under the seventh. If

THE SEVENTH TRUMP

were to make a sound on the air, it would be out of harmony with the other six of the series. That it covers "the great day of his wrath"—the time of judgments upon *the kingdoms of the world*—the pouring out of the "seven vials" of his wrath—the "time of trouble such as was not since there was a nation"—seems evident, for we are told, in the same sentence, of the wrath of God coming on the nations.—Rev. xi, 15, 18.

We see, then, that the *sounding* of the trumpets, and so coming in *like manner*, do not conflict, but rather add force to the fact that he comes "unawares," "as a thief," and steals away from the world "his treasure—his jewels." Remember, too, that this is Christ the spiritual body, that could not be seen without a miracle; that was present, yet unseen, during thirty-three days after his resurrection.

But will the world not see the saints when gathered or gathering? No; they are changed (in the twinkling of an eye) from Natural to Spiritual bodies, like unto Christ's glorious body, and in the instant of their change will be as invisible as he and angels. But those who arise from their graves? No; they were sown (buried) natural bodies; they are raised spiritual bodies—*invisible*. Won't the world see the graves open and the tombstones thrown down? A spiritual body (remember, we are comparing spiritual things with spiritual, not natural) coming out of the grave will not make any more of a hole in the ground than Christ's spiritual body made in the door when he came and stood in their midst, "the doors being shut."—John xx, 19, 26. But do not forget that only the Church are raised *spiritual* bodies—all others, *natural* fleshly bodies, as Lazarus, etc.

PRESENCE OF CHRIST BEFORE THE RAPTURE OF THE CHURCH.

Christ's personal presence and ministry of three and a half years at the first advent, as well as the three and a half years which followed his ministry, is termed "*the Harvest.*" It was the harvesting of the Jewish or Law age. Christ was present as the chief reaper—his disciples as under-reapers. Their work was separating of wheat from chaff, and the gathering of the wheat into the higher or Gospel dispensation. That harvest was the end of that age. Jesus said to his disciples, "Lift up your eyes and look on the fields, for they are white already to harvest." "I send you to reap that whereon ye bestowed no labor; other men (the prophets) have labored and ye are entered into their labors."—John iv, 38. That work was not general, nor for the world. He confined his labors to Judea, and the work to them did not cease until five days before his death, when he rode on the ass into the city, wept over it, gave them up, and said: "Your house is left unto you desolate." After his resurrection he sends the disciples to "preach the Gospel to every creature, beginning at Jerusalem." Nor were they suffered to preach to the world in general until the seven years of harvest-work to that Jewish people was fully accomplished, as God had promised.—Daniel ix, 27. "He (Jesus, chief reaper) shall confirm the covenant with many for one week" (seven years), in the midst of the week making all sacrifice to cease—by offering himself the true sacrifice. But the harvest or reaping done in the end of the Jewish age was confined to them as a people. The oracles of God had been committed to them as a people; wheat was sought among them, but as a nation they proved to be mainly chaff. The wheat was garnered (brought into the Gospel church) and the chaff burned (nation destroyed), and thus their harvest ended.

During the Gospel age, the church does not reap, but sows the seed. Paul plants, Apollos waters, God gives increase, etc. But there is to be a harvest in the end of this age, as *illustrated* in the parable of the tares and wheat, and *taught* in the explanation of the same.—Matt. 13. Notice that both wheat and tares are in the kingdom of heaven—the church—and that this parable, as also the other six of the series, relating to "the kingdom of heaven"—*the church*—refers not to the non-professing world, but to two classes *in* the church.

The Son of Man planted the church pure, good seed. During the days of the apostles there were special "gifts of the Spirit," such as "discerning of spirits," etc., by which they were able to prevent *tares* from getting in among the *wheat*—hypocrites getting into the church,—(instance, I Cor. v, 3.—"Simon Magus" —"Anannias and Sapphira," etc.); but when the apostles were dead, "while men slept," the enemy began to sow tares among the wheat. Paul says that the mystery of iniquity had begun to work even in his day; now they grow side-by-side in all the churches. Shall we separate them, Lord? No; we might make some mistake, pull up wheat and leave tares. "Let both grow together until *the Harvest.*" "The harvest *is* the end of the world," [*aion*-age.] "In the time of harvest I will say unto the reapers—the reapers are the angels—gather together. *first* the tares, and bind them in bundles to burn them; but gather the wheat into my barn."

Notice, this *Harvest* is the end of this age, yet, like the one ending, the Jewish age, it is a period of time—"In the *time* of harvest." Secondly, there is order—"Gather *first* the tares." There will come a time, then, in the end of this age, when the reapers—angels—will be present doing some sort of a separating work in the Church, yet an invisible presence and work. If the work of binding, gathering, etc., were a visible work by visible agents, two would not be found in the field, mill and bed when the hour for translation comes and the one is taken and the other left.—Matt. xxiv, 41.

Again, before the living are gathered, the *dead in Christ* must have risen, whether it be but a moment before; "the dead in Christ rise *first*—*then* we which are alive," etc.—I Thess. iv, 16. This harvest is not of the living only, but also of "the dead in Christ," "those that sleep in Jesus." The angels gather the living, but our Lord, who is the chief reaper here (as he was in the Jewish harvest), gathers or raises the dead. "I will raise him up;" "I am the resurrection and the life;" and in harmony with this thought we find that in Rev. xiv, 15—"One like unto the Son of Man, seated on a cloud," reaps the earth. (Here, two harvests, or two parts of one harvest, are shown; the second being the casting of the "vine of the earth" into the wine-press of his wrath—time of trouble.) The special point to which your attention is called, however, is the fact that this harvest will go on without outward demonstration, the chief and under-reapers being present but unseen.

Some may have confounded these remarks on the presence of Christ in a spiritual body with the presence of the spirit of Christ, but they are quite distinct. The latter never left the church; consequently, in that sense, he could not "come again." Of his spiritual presence he said: "Lo, I am with you alway, even unto the end of the world"—age. We refer to the *personal presence* which did go away, and was to come again—a spiritual *body*.

The Greek word generally used in referring to the second advent—*parousia*, frequently translated *coming*—invariably signifies *personal presence*, as having come, arrived, and never signifies *to be on the way*, as we use the word *coming*. This fact is recognized by many who are looking for the Lord; but the error under which the church in general is laboring, is that of supposing that *presence* implies *sight*—manifestation—appearance. In the Greek, however, other words are used to express revelation, appearing and manifestation, viz.: *phaneroo*—rendered shall appear in "When he shall *appear*, etc." and *apokalupsis*—rendered, shall be revealed in II Thes. i, 7. "When the Lord Jesus shall be revealed."

These and other texts teach us that our Lord will *reveal* or *manifest* himself to the world in such a manner that "Every eye shall see—[*optomai*—recognize] him"—"Be revealed in flaming fire," [judgments]. But what we now claim is, that before he is thus revealed, he will be *present unseen*, (by all except the Bride, who will see—recognize him—because of the eyes of her understanding being *opened* by the anointing of truth—see Eph. i, 17-19), doing a work and gathering his Bride, or body, to himself.

We have Christ's own words to prove that he will be present in the world, and the world for a time will know not of it. In Matt. xxiv, 37, we read: "As the days of Noah were, so shall also the *parousia* (*presence*) of the Son of Man be." The presence of Christ is not compared to the flood, but to the days of Noah, the days that were *before* the flood, as verse 38 shows; as then they ate, drank, married, etc., and *knew not*, so shall also the presence of the Son of Man be. The resemblance here mentioned is that of *not knowing*—they will *not know* of the *presence* of Christ. They may have been wicked then, and doubtless were, and may be similarly wicked *in his presence;* but wickedness is not the point of comparison; as then they ate, drank, married—proper enough things to be doing, not sins; so shall it be in Christ's presence. Now look at Luke xvii, 26, "As it was in the days of Noah, so shall it be also *in the days* of the Son of Man." Verse 27 tells us how it was in the days of Noah, they were eating, drinking, marrying, etc. "So shall it be *in the days* of the Son of Man." Surely the days of the Son of Man are not *before his days*, any more than the days of Henry Clay could be days before he was born. No, the more we examine the more we are convinced that the world will go on as usual, and *know not* until the "harvest is past, the summer ended," and they are not in the ark, not with the little flock "accounted worthy to escape," the time of trouble coming upon the world.— Luke xxi, 36. There will be no *outward demonstration*, until the church is gathered, whenever that takes place—soon or in the distant future.

We think we have good solid reasons, not imaginations, nor dreams, nor visions, but Bible evidences that we are now "in the days of the Son of Man:" that "the day of the Lord" has come, and Jesus, a spiritual body, *is present*, harvesting the Gospel age; yet, as he has said, the world seeth him no more; they eat, drink, etc., and "know not." This day of the Lord in which "he will show who is that blessed and only potentate, the Lord of Lords, and King of Kings," is already dawning, but the majority of the church, as well as the world, are asleep; and to them—the day "so cometh as a thief in the night." "But ye, brethren, are *not in darkness*, that that day should come upon *you* as a thief." "We are not of the night, therefore let us not sleep *as do others*." Not the worldly-wise, but those humble ones, wise from heavenly instruction, are meant when it is written, "the wise shall understand." But "if thou shalt *not watch* thou shalt *not know* what hour I will come upon thee." "Take heed lest *your* hearts be *over*charged with . . . . the cares of this life, and so that day come upon YOU *unawares*."—Luke xxi, 34.

We have seen that in his days of presence it will be as it was in Noah's days—the world will *know not.*—Matt. xxiv, 37; Luke xvii, 26. We are told that the day of the Lord is a day of trouble, *a day of clouds*, and thick darkness—Zeph. i, 15; Joel ii, 2. We are told also that "as the lightning which shineth," (not as the shining, but as the *invisible* electric fluid which causes the shining) "so shall the Son of Man *be in his day.*"—Matt. xxiv, 27; Luke xvii, 24. Now if he is to be as *lightning*, and his day *a day of clouds*, as the above texts assert, are they not in harmony? In the natural storm when we see flashes from lightning and hear peals of thunder, it gives evidence to us that atmospheric changes are taking place, and that the vitiated and corrupt "*air*" is to be changed, and we rejoice that it will be pure after the storm.

We now find a harmony in the account of our gathering. As we found "the voice of the archangel" and "the trump of God" were symbols of the closing epoch of this age and its troublous events, so now we find "*the clouds*" to symbolize the gathering of the trouble in that epoch; "*the lightning*" to symbolize or illustrate our Lord's presence "in his day," and that "*air*" is used as the symbol of the *spiritual throne* from which Satan ("the prince of the power of the *air*,") is to be deposed, and to which our Lord and his joint heirs are to come.

The great time of trouble, as a storm, has been, and continues gathering over earth. The air, in which Satan, "the prince of this world (age,) rules, becomes more and more vitiated until the storm breaks. The prince of darkness now works in the hearts of the children of disobedience to the accomplishment of his own will, viz., in oppressing and opposing justice and truth to the affliction of mankind. The clouds are gathering, and men's hearts are beginning to fail for fear of the approaching storm—"for fear of those things that are coming on the earth." Soon it will break in all its fury. But though it fills all hearts with fear and dread, in its final results it will prove a great blessing to the earth, (mankind,) displacing the present "powers of the air," ("powers of darkness,"—"spiritual wickedness in high (controlling) places,")—and giving place to earth's rightful ruler—Jesus and his Bride, also spiritual beings (powers of the *air.*)

So, after the storm, shall the "Sun of righteousness arise with healing in his wings," and the kingdom of darkness shall give place to the kingdom of light, and mankind will rejoice in the pure air and cloudless sunlight of that perfect day.

Notice, also, that all the flashes of lightning come from among the clouds, and become more and more vivid as the storm increases. How the various Scriptures interpret each other: "As the lightning, so shall the Son of Man be in his day." "Behold he cometh with *clouds.*" "The day of the Lord is a day of trouble, *of clouds* and thick darkness." "He maketh *the clouds* his chariot."

We conclude, then, that if "he cometh with clouds" of trouble, etc., we shall be "caught away in clouds" [*diaglott*] of the same sort, *after* he has thus come. If prepared, we shall be caught to meet him *during the gathering* of the trouble, before the storm bursts.

David [*anointed*] was doubtless a type of the church in her deliverance, as pictured in the song (II Sam. xxii,) in which he says (vs. 10): "He bowed the heavens also and came down and darkness was under his feet . . . . He was seen upon the wings of the wind, and he made darkness his pavilions round about him . . . . and thick clouds of the skies . . . . He sent forth and took me; . . . . He delivered me from the strong enemy" [death]. —Luke xxi, 36. Yes, our Lord when he has come and made trouble and darkness his pavilion, takes his Bride—delivers her from the strong enemy of the fleshily nature, death, into the perfection of the new divine nature—like unto Christ's *glorious body*. Lord help us to be ready for the change that we may be thus "caught away."

> " Forever with the Lord,
> Amen, so let it be;
> Life from the dead is in the word—
> "Tis immortality."

SPIRITUALISM.

WHEREVER we find a counterfeit we may rest assured there exists a genuine. If there were no genuine gold dollars, there could be no base imitations or counterfeits. Then, too, the base or spurious article must appear *very much like the genuine*, or it would not be a counterfeit.

This is what we claim relative to what is at the present time called "Spiritualism"—that it is a counterfeit of the true, as taught in the Bible.

Whoever has carefully searched the Scriptures cannot have failed to see that, while God throughout all past ages has condemned evil and sin in their various forms, and warned his children, both "Israel after the flesh" and also the spiritual children (the Gospel age Church), of the danger and bad results of evil, yet he has nevertheless permitted evil and good to stand side-by-side before the people for their choice. If we take heed to his Word we may discern which is evil, and, by obedience to that Word, shun the evil and choose the good.

God is the head and fountain of goodness and truth, and the Scriptures teach that Satan is the head and fountain of all evil and error—"the father of lies" (deceptions). Both of these are *spiritual* beings. "God is a spirit," and Satan, as we have heretofore shown, was once an angel of God—the chief or prince of "those angels which kept not their first (sinless) estate." These, though cast out from God's presence, are not yet destroyed; they still possess their angelic nature, though through sin they have become evil "*angels;*" consequently they still are *spiritual beings* (not human), and have the same powers as they ever had, and as good angels have, except that God has put them under certain limitations and restraints which we shall more fully discuss farther along.

If we trace them through the Scriptures we shall find that these *fallen spiritual beings* have continually made use of their spiritual—supernatural—powers to lead mankind astray into disobedience of God and injury to themselves.

Spiritual beings, as we have heretofore shown, possess powers greater and higher than humanity. We have seen, from the statements relative to good angels, that they can be present in our midst without our being conscious of their presence. (The angel of the Lord encampeth round about them that fear him.—Ps. xxxiv, 7. Are they not all ministering spirits sent forth to minister for those who shall be heirs of salvation?—Heb. i, 14.)

These, we have seen, have power to appear *as a flame of fire* (the angel of the Lord so appeared to Moses in the bush.—Gen. iii, 2), and they can and have *appeared as men.*

Some other powers of angels can be discovered by examining the record; for instance, the angels who delivered Lot and his family from Sodom had power to smite the rioters of Sodom with blindness.—Gen. xix, 11. An angel "did wondrously before Manoah;" another performed a miracle before Gideon.—Judges vi, 21, and 13-19. The angel of the Lord delivered the apostles from prison, and yet left the prison-doors unmolested; again, an angel delivered Peter from prison, the doors opening of their own accord.—Acts v, 19-23, and xii, 8. On many occasions they made known to men things which were about to come to pass, etc.

Now, the evil angels—"the devil and his angels"—have by nature the very same powers, but are restrained. So much of evil as can be overruled for good, and tend to the development of experience and the education and discipline of the "heirs of God, joint heirs with Jesus Christ"—is permitted, and the remainder *restrained*. As God through his Spirit and influence works in and through men who give themselves up to his control, so does Satan operate in and through those who "*yield themselves* as instruments of unrighteousness unto sin." "His servants ye are to whom you render *service*." As Jesus said to some, "Ye are of your father the devil, *for his works ye do*."

As "God in times past spake unto the fathers through the prophets," who were his mouthpieces, so Satan spake through his agents and agencies. His first agent was the serpent—it became his agent in beguiling Eve into disobedience. Satan manifested his powers *through* the Magicians and Soothsayers of Babylon, and remarkably in those of Egypt, where *God's powers* were manifested *through* Moses and Aaron before Pharaoh, while Satan's powers, of a similar kind, were used to *oppose* the truth for a time. Here these *two spiritual powers* were strikingly manifested; both did miracles—things which men alone could not do, but which men *possessed* of evil and good powers did do.—Exod. vii, 11-22, and viii, 7-18. "There were *false* prophets also among the people," who evidently spoke by an *inspiration*, or power in them almost like the real prophets of God; these were the counterfeits. (See II Peter ii, 1; Jer. xxiii, 21.)

We are aware that to the worldly mind it seems superstitious to believe that men and women may be so given over of themselves to Satan, and so controlled by him as to be wizards and witches; but they are recognized as such in the Scriptures, and we believe it. Israel was commanded to put such to death.— Exod. xxii, 18; Lev. xx, 27, etc. Manasseh, king of Judah, made Judah to err, etc.; he "used enchantments and used *witchcraft*, and dealt with a *familiar spirit* and with wizards."— II Chron. xxxiii, 6.

Take a concordance and see how much God says against wizards, witches, and "they that have familiar spirits"—*mediums* of the devil for communication with mankind. It was the claim of these *mediums* of "familiar spirits" that they held communication with the dead and received their information from them. In this claim they contradicted the plain statements of God's Word, which assure us that the *dead could not* furnish any information. (See Job xiv, 10-21; Eccl. ix, 10.)

But this was merely another way in which Satan sought to continue the lie imposed upon Eve in Eden. ["He is a *liar* from the beginning," said Jesus.] God had said that if disobedient they should *die*. Satan contradicted this statement—claimed that man had naturally Immortality, and could not die, and that God was a liar. Ever since, he seeks to uphold the statement, "Ye shall *not* surely die." Full well does he know that if people realized that it was the "spirits of demons" who spoke to them through the mediums, they would shun them; hence the claim that it is dead people (not *dead*, but more *alive* than ever) who communicate the information.

An illustration of this sort is given in I Saml. 28. Saul, king of Israel, had become wicked, and God would no longer communicate with him through the prophets. He was engaged in a war with the Philistines, and a great battle was about to be fought. He wanted council and desired to know what would be the outcome. Since the Lord would not answer him, he sought out one of the condemned and forbidden class, a *medium*, a woman who had a familiar spirit—the witch at Endor.

All are familiar with the story, (I Saml. xxviii, 3-20), how that the *medium* pretends ignorance as to her visitor, knows what Saul desires, gives a description of Samuel, etc. Then follows an account of the coming defeat of Saul's army and the death of himself and his sons. The fact that these things occurred just as foretold by the *medium*, has been thought by some to be a proof that Samuel really furnished the information. But, Satan could foretell those things as well as Samuel could were he alive. Not that Satan is a prophet, nor that God reveals coming things to him, but he is a student of God's Word and a *believer* of it. "Devils also believe and tremble."—Jas. ii, 19. The defeat of Saul and accession of David to the throne had been foretold by the prophet and both Saul and Satan knew it, and Satan had learned that every word of God is *sure*.

Besides we should not forget the words of the apostle, that he that hath the power of death is the devil.—Heb. ii. 14. Since he is executor of the death penalty, and must have the permission to execute from God, (Job i, 12), is it strange that he knew that he was to have power over the lives of Saul, his sons, and many others on the next day? No, it is the *reasonable* inference. Certainly we should not for a moment suppose that God (or -Samuel, *if he could*) would recognize, or use any means of communication which he had prohibited on pain of death, and condemned as wicked. Read I Chron. x, 13.

Coming further down the stream of time, we learn that the same wicked spirits continued to operate in the same manner. The Lord, while still permitting them, warns the people against such, saying, "they shall say unto you, 'seek unto them that have familiar spirits (spirit *mediums*) and unto wizards that peep and mutter.' (But) should not a people seek unto their God? For [why should] the living [go] to the dead? To the law and to the testimony, [the Bible], if they speak not according to this *Word* it is because there is no light in them."—Isa. viii, 19. God warns people not to believe any one whose teachings are contrary to the *Word*, no matter what powers they may exercise.

Coming down to the days of Jesus and the apostles, we find

that Satan still operated in much the same manner, as well as a variety of other ways. Among the more notable instances [not to mention the numerous cases of casting out of devils, etc., by both Jesus and the disciples] we might remind you of the experience of Philip and Peter with Simon the sorcerer.—Acts viii, 7, 9-24. "Unclean spirits crying with loud voice came out of many that were *possessed;* .... but there was a certain man named Simon which .... used sorcery and bewitched the people .... to whom they all gave heed .... saying, this man is the great power (*medium*) of God." Thus did Satan use *his power* to delude the people.

Paul and Barnabas had an experience with another of these *mediums* of the devil, named Elymas, who withstood them. Paul addressing him said, "O full of all subtilty and all mischief, thou child of the devil, thou enemy of all righteousness, wilt thou not cease to *pervert the right ways* of the Lord?"—Acts xiii, 10. And he was blinded immediately. Again, Paul and Silas met a female *medium* at Phillippi. "A certain damsel *possessed* with a spirit of divination .... which brought her masters much gain by soothsaying." But Paul "turned and said to the spirit [Satan] I command thee in the name of Jesus Christ to come out of her. And he came out the same hour."—Acts xvi, 16, 18.

And so ever since, Satan has kept up his practices with various changes of method to suit the circumstances; sometimes with characteristic devilishness, at other times in the garb of religion, "for Satan himself is transformed into an angel of light, therefore it is no great thing if his ministers [*mediums*] also be transformed as ministers of righteousness."—II Cor. xi, 14. In our day, when knowledge is so great, and morality (called *Christianity*) so popular, Satan *must*, if he would continue to oppose truth, take the religious cloak; and so he does. To-day Spiritualism ranks itself among the religious sects. ["The synagogue [church] of Satan," truly.]

Spiritualism, though refined and modernized, is yet the same that it ever was, in ages past. Its object is not the inculcation of truth, nor of love for God the Father and our Lord Jesus Christ. They claim that Jesus was a fine *medium* and taught and used spiritualism in his day as well as he understood it. They do not outwardly profess to oppose the Bible and its teachings, but they do so really, both teaching and practicing the very things therein condemned, and still seeking to prove by their enchantments that men are not *dead*, thus endeavoring to uphold Satan's first falsehood.—Gen. iii, 4.

They still possess supernatural powers, too, just as in the days of Saul, and Paul, and Moses. While we do not question that some of the things claimed to be done are mere deceptions, yet we know of many things done by them, where no deception was possible. Among those who believe "*in this way*" we know of several who once were *mediums* of the devil and did "those things whereof they are now ashamed." These, when coming to a knowledge of the truth, are thankful for their escape from that "snare of the devil." Spiritualism hates the light, and their wonders are done under cover of their favorite principle—*darkness*. Their work of proselyting, too, is dark, covered—secret. Jesus gives us a word of wisdom on this subject. "Every one that doeth evil hateth the light, neither cometh to the light lest his deeds should be reproved."—Jno. iii, 20.

Though working stealthily, their numbers are large and embrace many of the influential of earth—judges, senators, etc. The queen of what is known as the greatest *Christian* kingdom of earth, on whose possessions the light of day is said never to set, called the "Christian Queen," is known by many to be a "Spiritualist." It is coming before people in a way that commands attention, and those who do not realize it to be the work of Satan, are almost sure to regard it as a power of God.

The Rev. Joseph Cook, justly celebrated for his able defense of the Bible and its Author, against the attacks of atheists and infidels, such as Huxley, Darwin, Arnold, *et al.*, has lately had his attention aroused to the recognition of the growing influence of "Spiritualism," and having investigated the subject to some extent, he recently delivered a lecture on the subject, in which he expressed his belief that many of their tricks and performances are done by no human power, and are actually *supernatural*. He does not pretend to say how, or by what power, but claims that not only himself, but some of the profoundest scientific minds of Germany have reached the conclusion that Spiritualism cannot be condemned as *false* by any scientific tests yet applied to it.

Nor is this power of Spiritualism difficult to account for if we take the Bible as our authority and recognize it as the work of Satan, whom Jesus designates "the prince of this world."—Jno. xiv, 30. "The prince of the power of the air (spiritual power) *the spirit* that now worketh in the children of disobedience."— Eph. ii, 2. And the same book is our authority for saying that "Spiritualism" has not yet reached the climax of its power; its powers are to increase wonderfully. Paul says, (I Tim. iv, 1,) "Now the spirit [of God] speaketh expressly that in the *latter times* some shall depart from the faith giving heed to seducing [deceiving] spirits and doctrines of devils." Jesus says, "They are the spirits of devils working miracles, which go forth unto the kings of the whole world to gather them to the battle of that great *day of God* Almighty."—Rev. xvi, 14.

Peter (ii, 4,) and Jude (vi,) tell us, that when cast out of God's presence as evil angels, they were bound by "chains of darkness" "unto the judgment of the great day." Many Scriptures have shown us that the closing part of the Gospel age is to be upon the living a time of trial and trouble, preparing them for the coming Millennial reign of Christ, and is called "the day of the Lord"—"the great day"—"the great day of his wrath," etc. We understand, then, that Satan and his angels have been limited; might not appear except through human beings who willingly gave themselves up to be "possessed of devils" or became his "*mediums*." He has thus been confined or chained. But we claim that this "*day of the Lord*"—day of the "*presence* of the Son of man"—has already commenced, that the Scriptures prove it to be so; and if the chains of darkness restrain Satan *until* "the great day," we should expect that very soon those chains will be loosed and no longer restrain. (Any who expect soon the loosing of those powers should, to be consistent, recognize both "the day of the Lord" and the *trial* as commenced.)

The facts correspond to this exactly. "Spiritualists" claim that they are having more power to show their wonders, daily; and they claim now (one case very recently) that the spirits can *materialize in broad daylight;* and they promise wonderful revelations and manifestations *very soon*. Now, materialization of a spiritual being, just as they claim, has been possible all along to the angels of God, of which we have many records—angels on many occasions appearing *as men*. Jesus, as we have seen, when *born of the Spirit* at his resurrection, a spiritual body, ("that which is born of the Spirit *is spirit*,") was, as all other spiritual beings, (good and evil) *invisible* to human sight, and in making known his resurrection to his disciples he appeared in various fleshly "forms" *materialized.*—Mark xvi, 12. These are the powers which Satan has desired, but could not heretofore use, because bound or limited, but which he will have when the judgment (trial) of "the day of the Lord" begins. (Which we believe is *now*.)

The trial of this "day" causes not only a "time of trouble" and distress among nations, but it includes a trouble or fire upon the living phase of the church. This church trouble comes first, and we believe began in the spring of 1878, and is to result in the purifying of faith; and will bring those who continue to bear the name of *Christian* to the firm foundations of the teachings of the *Word of God*. For all *the errors* of human traditions shall be consumed as dross, wood, hay, stubble, in the *fire* (trial) of this day. The apostle says, "think it not strange concerning the fiery trial which *shall try you* (the church) as though some strange [unforetold] thing happened unto you."—I Pet. iv, 12. For the fire of that day shall try every man's work of what sort it is: "He that hath built [his faith] with gold, silver, and precious stones [the truths of God's Word] the same shall remain. (His faith will not be destroyed.) But if any man build with wood, hay, stubble, (the teachings and creeds of *man*,) the same shall suffer loss, etc.—I Cor. iii, 12–15.

This trial is "the trial of your faith," and in this "day of the Lord" not only does the light of truth shine *strongly and beautifully*, showing us the great prize of our high calling as we never saw it before; revealing to us the *present King*, who causes us to sup with him and feeds us with his truth which is "meat in due season," giving strength needed in *this* day; but it is also a day for the increase of the powers of evil, that the separation between the wheat and tares (the children of the kingdom and the children of the wicked one, Matt. xiii, 38,) may be complete.

Because of this struggle between truth and error, the *real* and the *false*, Spiritualism, etc., Paul says, "My brethren, be strong in the Lord and the power of his might. Put on the whole armor of God that ye may be *able* to stand against the wiles of the devil. For we wrestle not against flesh and blood [not against human beings, but against evil *spiritual* beings] but against principalities, against powers, against the *rulers of the darkness* of this world, (Satan—the prince of this world)—Jno. xiv, 30, against *spiritual* wickedness in high (controlling) places. *Wherefore*, [on this account] take unto you the whole armor of God, that ye may be able to withstand [the *spiritual* wickedness—the devil's wiles] in the *evil day* [this day of the Lord's presence—day of trial.] .... Stand, therefore, having your loins girt about with *truth* and having on the breastplate of righteousness, etc." —Eph. vi, 11–14.

This same day of trial is referred to in Psalm xci, where only those who have made God's "truth their shield and buckler [support] are able to withstand the *snares* of the devil, the '*arrows*' of infidelity, and the moral '*pestilence*' of Spiritualism, while thousands shall *fall* at their side."

"In God I have found a retreat,
  Where I can securely abide;
No refuge, nor rest so complete,
  And here I intend to reside.

"The pestilence walking about,
  When darkness has settled abroad,
Can never compel me to doubt
  The presence and power of our Lord.

"A thousand may fall at my side,
  Ten thousand at my right hand,—
Above me his wings are spread wide.
  Beneath them in safety I stand.

"His truth is my buckler and shield,
  His love he hath set upon me;
His name on my heart he hath sealed,—
  E'en now his salvation I see."
        Songs of the Bride.

There are portions of Scripture which *seem* to teach that during this "Day of the Lord" there will be manifestations of the saints *as men* in fleshly bodies—those who have been *changed* to spiritual bodies like unto Christ's glorious body—and that they will *appear* as he "appeared" after his resurrection, and do a work of teaching as he taught the disciples, opening men's understandings that they might understand the Scriptures.

We have seen that the coming of Moses, the first and second times, to deliver Israel from Egypt, was a type of the two comings of the Lord. The second time he came with *power*, and "Aaron, the saint," was his mouthpiece before Pharaoh—during the signs, etc. So we expect, that the living representatives of the church, will sometime be used as the mouthpieces of their Lord before the world [Egypt in type]. As there in type Jannes and Jambres, and the other magicians under Satanic power, opposed and hindered for a time the effect of the wonderful powers wrought through Aaron, so we anticipate that in the antitype, when the living church is used as the Lord's mouthpiece, they will be withstood and their teachings controverted by the same *spiritual wickedness*—"Spiritualism"—which will seek to do the same things and *partly* be able. Paul seems to refer directly to this in II Tim. iii, 1-8, when, after saying, "In the last days [of the age] perilous times shall come," etc., he adds: "Now, as Jannes and Jambres withstood Moses, so do these also resist the truth . . . . but they shall proceed no further; for their *folly* shall be manifest unto all men as theirs also was."

We suggest again, then, that every counterfeit is a proof of a *genuine;* second, that none but valuable things are counterfeited; and third, that a counterfeit must resemble the genuine very *closely*, or it would not deceive. Already, Spiritualists are talking much as we do, of "the good time coming," the "glorious day," and even declare that Jesus is *present*, etc. This is an old practice with our opponent. At the first advent the devils knew Jesus, and, crying out, said: "Thou art Christ, the Son of God;" and he, rebuking them, suffered them not to speak, "for they knew that he was Christ."—Luke iv, 41. (See also Paul's experience, Acts xvi, 17.) Yes, "the devils also believe and tremble."—James ii, 19. And no doubt they would fain call some of us Spiritualists, both for the purpose of bringing to their credit our knowledge of God's Word and plan, and to seek to offset the value and effect of our *Bible* teaching, by claiming us as one with themselves.

But, beloved, "believe not every spirit, but try the spirits whether they be *of God*" or of Satan. "By their fruits ye shall know them." That system, by whatsoever name it calls itself, whose time and talent is spent in doing useless and foolish things, and making use of supernatural power to obtain money; which appeals merely to the human *credulity*, and neither seeks nor develops an increase of faith and love toward God and men; ignores Jesus and the plan of salvation; repudiates the Bible; whose tendency is *toward* things earthly, sensual, devilish—

"Free-loveism," etc.—is *not of God*, but bears unmistakable signs of Satan being its author.

On the contrary, a system based not on forbidden and *pretended* communications with the *dead*, but upon the Word of God only; whose teachings tend to the glory of both the Father and his Son, our Lord; which seeks to unfold to those who have "ears to hear" and "eyes to see" the glorious beauty and grandeur of God's plan of salvation, of which Jesus is the recognized foundation; which tends not to the ignoring of any part of the Word, but to a searching of the Scriptures daily; which tends *toward* and teaches that the prize of our high calling is obtainable only by patient perseverance in well-doing—the death of the *old* nature and newness of life as a *new creature in Christ Jesus*, bears unmistakably the stamp of God, and *is of God*— for it speaks according to his Word.

PART IV.

THE DAY OF JUDGMENT.

VERY confused notions are held by many as to the work of judgment in the future age. The popular idea on the subject being something like this:
The Father, robed as a judge, with stern aspect, is seated on a great white throne. By his side stands the Saviour with loving eyes and pleading face. The world of mankind is marshaled before him. They come up in close ranks, and with downcast faces toward the Judge. The very large majority are commanded to depart toward the left. Trembling with despair they hurry away, and are at once seized by a guard of demons, and swiftly dragged, shrieking with terror, down—down—down. In the advancing throng, there comes now and then *one*, who is at once recognized by the Saviour as a true Christian, and introduced to the Father as such, who welcomes him to the right hand, where he is immediately crowned, and seated with the angels to view the remainder of the solemn scene. This separating work is to continue until all who have ever lived have passed the tribunal; the whole period of time occupied being something less than twenty-four hours, thus constituting "the day of judgment." The greater number of these, it is generally thought, have already been once judged (at death) and allotted to their final destiny in heaven or hell, but for some inconceivable reason they are brought again before the judgment seat, and are again remanded to their former condition.

While some features of this picture are drawn from symbolic Bible imagery, the conception as a whole is very far from being a scriptural one. As to the gathering of the world before the Judge in a kind of military review, and the immediate separation of the classes, while it is the likeness in the figure, it is of necessity as far from the real as a type is from its antitype.

THREE GREAT PERIODS OF SEPARATION

are, we think, clearly revealed in God's Word: "The separation of the chaff from the wheat," Matt. iii, 10, 12; "the tares from the wheat," Matt. xiii, 37, 43; and "the sheep from the goats," Matt. xxv, 31.

The first separation is in the past, occurring in the "harvest," or end of the Jewish (*aion*) age. Jesus himself, while on earth, thoroughly purged the floor of the Jewish house, gathered the wheat into the Gospel church, and cast the chaff into a fire, which, culminating at the destruction of Jerusalem, burns even yet against the Jew. So far from marshaling that nation in rank and file before him, they were not even aware of the test then made, and were condemned because they *knew not* the time of their visitation.—Luke xix, 44.

The second great separation was due to take place at the end of this *aion* [age], *i. e.*, closing period of the Gospel dispensation. This work has actually been going on in our midst, and the world and worldly church know nothing of it. So in the last great harvest in the age of judgment: God's truth, the two-edged sword, will quietly, but surely, do the dividing work; and that Word not spoken but written, will plainly manifest the sheep and the goats.

THE TERM "DAY"

in Bible times, as now, was frequently used to cover a long but definite period; as, for instance, "The *day*" in which "Jehovah God made the earth and the heavens." Gen. ii, 4. "The *day* of the temptation in the wilderness." Heb. iii, 8. [40 years.] "The *day* of salvation." II Cor. vi, 2. [Gospel dispensation.]

As to the period comprised in "the day of judgment," if the student will but faithfully use a reference Bible or a concordance, and find the *amount* and *kind* of work to be accomplished "in that day," he will soon be glad to accept of Peter's explanation of it, that "one day is with the Lord as a thousand years;" and believing the Revelation of Jesus Christ, rejoice in the promise there given, to "reign with him a thousand years." As to

THE KIND OF JUDGING

which is to be carried on, we must consult the Word if we would get the truth. Turn to the book of "Judges," and we find that after the death of Joshua, the Israelites forsook Jehovah, and worshipped Baal. To bring them to their senses, their enemies were allowed to triumph over them. When they repented, "Jehovah raised up *judges*, who delivered them out of the hand of those that spoiled them." For instance, "When the children of Israel cried unto Jehovah, Jehovah raised up a *deliverer* Othniel. And the spirit of Jehovah came upon him, and he *judged* Israel, and went out to war, and prevailed, and the land had rest for forty years," until Othniel died. Thus it continued through the period of the judges until Samuel, who "*judged Israel all the days of his life.*" When Samuel had grown old, the Elders of Israel asked him for "a *King* to *judge us* like all the nations."—I Sam. viii, 5, 20.

A *judge* then, in those days, was a person eagerly sought after; a *ruler* to be desired; who would deliver his people from oppression, administer justice to the wronged, and bring peace and joy to those over whom he exercised authority.

The world, and even the Church, at the present day, led astray by an unscriptural theology, puts far away the idea of Christ's *presence* to judge [rule] the world as something to be dreaded by all. Not so the heaven inspired prophets of old. To them it was one grand and glorious epoch, for which, as Paul said, "creation groaneth."

Listen to David and the sweet singers of Israel, in the first psalm sung by the first divinely-appointed choir, at the home-bringing of the ark:

> " Let the heavens be glad,
> And let the earth rejoice:
> And let men say among the nations, Jehovah reigneth.
> Let the sea roar, and the fullness thereof:
> Let the fields rejoice, and all that are therein.
> Then shall the trees of the wood sing aloud,
> At the PRESENCE of JEHOVAH,
> BECAUSE HE COMETH
> TO JUDGE THE EARTH.
> O give thanks unto Jehovah, for he is good,
> FOR HIS MERCY ENDURETH FOREVER."

We might multiply quotations like the above, but they ought to be familiar to the faithful student of the Word.

WHY

did "all the holy prophets since the world began" long for "that day" when the Anointed should be present to rule, to reign, to judge?

WHY does all Christendom of this age shrink at the bare mention of that day? Because they do not comprehend the nature of the work of that day, nor the grandeur of its results, while the prophets spoke as they were moved by the Holy Spirit of God, who knew what he himself had planned and purposed.

IN "THE DAY OF THE LORD,"

as in the days of creation, there is an evening and a morning. So the Jews kept their time: beginning their day with evening. It is God's order—first the cross, then the crown. The night was forty years long to the children of Israel. To the Gospel church it has been many centuries. So the nations in the coming age must first run the race before they receive the prize for which they run. And during their trial, as in ours, there must be "weeping for a night; but joy cometh in the morning."

Many, who have failed to "*search* the Scriptures,' as commanded, have seen only this night of darkness; and it has hung before them like a funeral pall, cutting off the light of glory beyond.

A DARK NIGHT

is indeed closing over a sleeping church and a blind world, during which many woes will be poured out upon them. But when they have well learned the lesson of obedience *through suffering*, as all past overcomers have, they reap a blessed reward.

The day of judgment, then, divides itself into two parts. First, a "time of trouble, ' during which the nations will be subdued, and humbled, and taught the lesson of Nebuchadnezzar their type, "that the Most High ruleth in the kingdom of men, and giveth it to whomsoever he will." Secondly, a morning, in which the Sun of righteousness will rise with healing in his wings, driving away the mists of ignorance and superstition; destroying the miasma of sin, and bringing light and life and love to the downtrodden sons of men. During the first-named period, such scriptures as the following have a fulfillment:

"Behold, the day of the LORD cometh, cruel both with wrath and fierce anger, to lay the land desolate: and he shall destroy the sinners thereof out of it For the stars of heaven and the constellations thereof shall not give their light; the sun shall be darkened in his going forth, and the moon shall not cause her light to shine. [Symbolical of a spiritual night.] And I will punish the world for their evil and the wicked for their iniquity; and I will cause the arrogancy of the proud to cease, and will lay low the haughtiness of the terrible."—Isa. xiii, 9, 11. "Ask of me, and I shall give thee the heathen for thine inheritance, and the uttermost parts of the earth for thy possession. Thou shalt break them with a rod of iron; thou shalt dash them in pieces like a potter's vessel."—Psa. ii, 8, 9.

Unquestionably the kingdoms of this world are loyal to their prince. They are mainly controlled by evil, selfish, corrupt men, the agents and representatives of the "Prince of darkness," who do his will.

When the *new Prince* takes control, the dominion is to be given into new hands, and the Lord proclaims: "I will overthrow the throne of kingdoms and I will destroy the kingdoms of the Gentiles."—Hag. ii, 22.

Thus by "breaking in pieces"—throwing down—"the kingdoms of this world become the kingdoms of our Lord and his Christ," who shall reign forever.—Rev. xi, 15. Under the new rule there will be new rulers, and we read, "The saints of the most High shall take the kingdom, (dominion) and possess the kingdom forever."—Daniel vii, 18. Again, "All nations, tongues, people, etc., shall serve and obey him." At present they do not, and they must be brought, by chastisement, to submission; and this is accomplished in "The day of the Lord." The overthrow of nations and society will necessarily involve *individual* trouble. But, "When the judgments of the Lord are in the earth the inhabitants of the world will learn righteousness."—Isa. xxvi, 9.

"That day is a day of wrath, a day of trouble and distress, a day of wasteness and desolation, a day of darkness and gloominess. I will bring distress upon men, and they shall walk like blind men, because they have sinned against the Lord. Neither their silver nor their gold shall be able to deliver them, in the day of the Lord's wrath."—Zeph. i, 15. "Therefore wait ye upon me, saith the Lord, until *the day* that I rise up to the prey: for my determination is to gather the nations, that I may assemble the kingdoms, to pour upon *them* mine indignation, even all my fierce anger: for all the earth shall be devoured with the *fire of my jealousy*. For then I will turn to the people a pure language, that they may all call upon the name of the Lord, to serve him with one consent."—Zeph. iii, 8. So extreme is the trouble here described, that the world is said to be *burned up* by the Lord's anger—yet it has a good effect, for after all the indignation against and destruction of governments, the people remain. [The destruction is one of governments,] and having experienced the misrule of the "Prince of this world" they are prepared to have the Lord take "his great power and rule," and to "serve the Lord with one consent."

Rev. vi, 15, figuratively describes that time of falling of kingdoms when every mountain (kingdom) and island shall be moved. The kings and chief ones, as well as bondmen, will recognize in this trouble that "the great day of his wrath is come," and will seek to make alliances and to hide themselves from the sure coming storm. They will seek to be covered and protected by the great mountains (kingdoms) of earth and to be hid in the great rocks of this world's societies, (Masonic, Odd-Fellows, etc.;) but *they* shall *not be able* to deliver them in the day of the Lord's anger, for "all the kingdoms of the world shall be thrown down," and instead of these mountains (kingdoms) "the kingdom of the Lord becomes *a great mountain*, and fills the whole earth."—Daniel ii, 35, 45. Malachi iv, 1 describes the coming day of trouble and sees the anger of the Lord there displayed—"the fire of God's jealousy." "Behold the day cometh, that shall burn as an oven; and all the proud, and all that do wickedly shall be stubble, and the day that cometh shall burn them up." Here the wicked are symbolized by stubble, God's wrath by fire, and the righteous by "calves of the stall." Vs. 2.

"The heathen raged, the kingdoms were moved: he uttered his voice, the earth melted; * * Come, behold the works of Jehovah, what desolations he hath made in the earth. He maketh wars to cease unto the ends of the earth: he breaketh the bow, and cutteth the spear in sunder; he burneth the chariot in the fire. Be still, and know that I am God: I will be exalted among the heathen, I will be exalted in the earth."—Psa. xlvi, 6, 10. How does he make wars to cease? Evidently by the "desolations" above mentioned. The nations will be so satiated with bloodshed; and by bitter experience, will so realize the misery of injustice, and oppression, and sin, that they will loathe themselves and their ways, and will willingly turn and seek for purity and peace. But to produce this effect, the command will first go forth: "Proclaim ye this among the Gentiles: Prepare war, wake up the mighty men, let all the men of war draw near; let them come forth:

BEAT YOUR PLOWSHARES INTO SWORDS,

and your *pruning hooks into spears:* let the weak say, I am strong."—Joel iii, 9, 10. The dreadful lesson of the exceeding sinfulness of sin, will be learned in time, and well learned, for "thy people shall be willing in the day of thy power."—Psa. cx, 3. Then after they have been brought to a condition of willingness to let "this man (the Christ of God) reign over them," we find as a result of his judgship, they shall

BEAT THEIR SWORDS INTO PLOWSHARES,

and their *spears into pruning hooks:* nation shall not lift up sword against nation, neither shall they learn war any more." —Isa. ii, 4.

The preceding verses tell us when this blessed time will come, and also other events in this glorious day of Christ's presence, as judge over all the earth. "It shall come to pass in the last days, that the mountain [government or kingdom] of the Lord's house, ['whose house are we'—Heb. iii, 6.] shall be in the top of the mountains, [place of power], and shall be exalted above the hills, [kingdoms of earth], and all nations shall flow unto it. And many people shall go and say, come ye, and let us go up to the MOUNTAIN of Jehovah, to the HOUSE of the God of Jacob; and he will teach us of his ways, and we will walk in his paths: for out of Zion [the New Jerusalem—heavenly government] shall go forth the *law* and the *word* of Jehovah from Jerusalem" [restored earthly Jerusalem and her priesthood.]—Isa. ii, 3.

At this time (end of "time of trouble,") the nations will have been subdued, and gladly they will submit to the righteous control of the new heavenly kingdom; and here is the introduction of the Millennial reign. Notice, they say: "Come, let us go up to the Mountain of the Lord,"—or, let us submit to the new kingdom of God,—"and he will teach us of his ways, and we will walk in his paths." After the terrible experience of the time of trouble, they will be glad to forsake their own ways. How gladly will they then learn that his "ways are ways of pleasantness, and all (*his*) *paths* are peace." Here will be the silver lining of that dark storm-cloud of the "day of wrath"— "When the judgments of the Lord are in the earth, the inhabitants of the world will learn righteousness."—Isa. xxvi, 9.

> " Behind a frowning Providence
> He hides a smiling face."

During the one thousand years thus introduced, Satan is bound, evil restrained, that the people may be deceived no more, and the Lord and his Bride (the saints), as kings and priests, shall rule and teach them. None need then say to his neighbor: Know thou the Lord? for all shall know him, from the least to the greatest. The way of life will then be so plain that the wayfaring man, though a fool, shall not err therein. Yes, God's Word will then be an open book to all the world, and all its present seeming contradictions will then shine forth as beautifully harmonious as they now do to us, who have come to understand the glorious plan of the ages.

A thousand years of such ruling and teaching! How it will lift from the redeemed world the curse—ignorance, misery and death; restoring perfection, harmony, peace and beauty. This thousand years is the time, during which all the nations are gathered before the judgment seat of Christ. It is their judgment day—one thousand years.

During all that time, God's truth, as a two-edged sword, will be quietly, but surely as now, doing a separating work, dividing the *sheep* from the *goats*.—Matth. xxv, 31-46. The great mass of mankind will learn God's ways, and delight to walk therein. These he calls his sheep—followers, and during the age they are gradually gathered to his right hand—place of favor—and in the end of the age the Lord thus addresses them: "Come ye blessed * * inherit the kingdom prepared *for you* from the foundation of the world."

The earthly kingdom or dominion was intended and prepared for human (earthly) beings. It was given originally to the earthly Adam. ["Let him have dominion over the beasts of the field, the fowl of heaven, and the fish of the sea."] He was to be the Lord of Earth, governing it in harmony with the heavenly government. This dominion he lost through disobedience and sin, and it passed under the control of "him that hath the power of death, that is, the devil"—the prince of this world, "*who now ruleth* in the hearts of the children of disobedience." This *dominion*, purchased or redeemed for mankind by Jesus (and his body,) is to be restored to them, when they have been restored to the perfect condition, where they shall again be in harmony with God's government, and be able to wisely exercise the governing power. To these the Lord will say, "Come, inherit the kingdom prepared *for you*." [Let no one confound this *earthly dominion* with the spiritual—heavenly kingdom inherited by Jesus and shared by his *Bride*—the overcomers of the Gospel Age. "To him that overcometh will I grant to sit with me in my throne."]

Why, say they, are we considered worthy of such honor? Because, replies the King, you have done good unto some of these —God's children—"my brethren"—your neighbors and brethren also—and thus have showed your ready obedience to the one great law of the heavenly kingdom which includes all others— Love. But there will be some, even in that glorious time of favor and blessing, who will not have *this man* (Christ) to rule over them, and who show their indisposition to do God's will by neglecting others and selfishly gratifying their own desires. But one will (the will of God) is to regulate and continually control the universe, and that will or law is expressed in one word—LOVE— for "God is Love," and "Love is the fulfilling of the Law."

During the Millennial reign Christ "puts all enemies under his feet"—puts down all rule, authority and power opposed to God, ultimately destroying "the goats:" "These shall go forth into *aionion* cutting off;" [death] (Matt. xxv, 46, Diaglott), *i. e.*, these shall be forever cut off from that life which they had a second time forfeited. They had been redeemed from the Adamic death by the precious blood of Christ, but having despised the privileges thereafter offered under his kingdom, "there remaineth henceforth no more sacrifice for sins." The destruction of Satan is due at the same time.—Rev. xx, 10 and 15.

Thus, with all things subjected to the will of God, the Son shall deliver up earth's dominion to God, even the Father, (I Cor. xv, 28), whose *will* then will be "in all," and done in earth as in heaven.

Then the first dominion, lost by Adam, will have been restored in the Second Adam, (the spiritual), and the *restored race* will be so in harmony with God as to rule their dominion in accordance with his law—LOVE.

A better illustration of man's dominion over earth, yet subservient to the laws of God's kingdom, cannot be made than that which is afforded in the government of this country. Each State is permitted to govern itself—make its own laws, etc., so long as it is in harmony with the government of the United States. Just so the dominion of Earth, which has been preparing for mankind since the foundation of the world, will be restored to him, when he is prepared to rule it in harmony with the heavenly kingdom—which kingdom is an everlasting kingdom, enduring throughout all generations.—Psa. cxlv, 13.

They shall have everlasting life, as Adam had it, viz., so long as they remain obedient to God's will, which will be *ever*, since they will have learned the evil effects of any other way than his.

With these thoughts of the "Day of Judgment" and its beneficial results to mankind, we are prepared to read intelligently Psalm xcvii, which we quote:—

"JEHOVAH REIGNETH;
Let the earth rejoice; let the multitude of isles be glad.
Clouds and darkness are round about him:
Righteousness and judgment [justice] the establishment of his throne.
A fire goeth before him,
And burneth up his enemies round about,
His lightning [truth] enlighteneth the world:
The earth [nations] saw and trembled.
The hills [earthly governments] melted like wax at the *presence* of Jehovah.
At the presence of the LORD of the whole earth.
The Heavens [immortalized saints in heavenly places] declare his righteousness, *and all the people see his glory.*
Zion heard and *was glad:*
And the daughters of Judah *rejoiced,*
Because of thy JUDGMENTS, O Jehovah."

WOULD THERE BE ROOM FOR THEM ON THE EARTH IF THE BILLIONS OF THE DEAD WERE RESURRECTED?

This is an important point. What if we should find that while the Bible asserts a resurrection for all men, by actual measurement they could not find a footing on the earth—what then? It is frequently asserted, by people who should know better, that the earth is one vast cemetery. Now let us see; figure it out for yourself and you will find this an error: you will find that there is room enough for the "*restitution of all things*, which God hath spoken by the mouth of all his holy prophets."—Acts iii, 21.

Let us, in this calculation, assume that it is six thousand years since the creation of man, and that there are one billion four hundred million people now living on the earth—(the largest estimate.) Our race began with *one pair*, but that none should think us illiberal, let us calculate that there were as many people then, as now—(one billion four hundred millions,) and further, that there never was less than that number at any time. (Actually the flood reduced the population to *eight* persons.)

Again we will be liberal and estimate *three* generations to a century, or thirty-three years to a generation, while, according to Gen. v, there were but eleven generations from Adam to the flood, a period of one thousand six hundred and fifty-six years, or about one hundred and fifty years to the generation.

Now let us see: six thousand years are sixty centuries; three generations to each would give us one hundred and eighty generations (since Adam.) One billion four hundred million to a generation would give two hundred and fifty-two billion as the total number of our race from creation until now, according to our *liberal* estimate, which is probably about *twice* the actual number.

Where shall we find room enough for this great multitude? Let us measure the land. The State of Texas (United States) contains two hundred and thirty-seven thousand square miles. There are twenty-seven million eight hundred and seventy-eight thousand four hundred square feet in a mile, and, therefore, six trillion six hundred and seven billion one hundred and eighty million eight hundred thousand square feet in Texas. Allowing ten square feet as the surface covered by each dead body, we find that Texas, as a cemetery, would at this rate hold six hundred and sixty billion seven hundred and eighteen million eighty thousand bodies, or nearly *three* times as many as we calculated had lived on the earth.

A person, standing, occupies about one and two-third square feet of space. At this rate the present population of the earth (one billion four hundred million) could *stand* on an area of eighty-six square miles; an area much less than that of the city of London, England, or the city of Philadelphia, United States. And the island of Ireland (area thirty-two thousand square miles) would furnish standing-room for more than twice the number of people who have ever lived on the earth, even at our liberal calculation.

PART V.

"THE CHRIST OF GOD."

THE word Christ or *Kristos* is a Greek word, introduced into our English language, but not *translated* into it. Its translation is, ANOINTED.

"Unto us a child is born," etc., and "they shall call his name Jesus." The name Jesus means Deliverer or Saviour, and the child was named in view of a work he was to do; for we are told, "he *shall* save his people from their sins." Jesus was always his name, but from the time of his baptism, when the Holy Ghost descended upon him and *anointed* him as the High Priest, preparatory to his making "the sin offering" on the cross, and thus accomplishing what is indicated by his *name*, his *title* has been "The Anointed,"—Jesus "the *Christ* (anointed) of God."—Luke ix, 20. [Compare Acts x, 37, 38.]

Jesus was frequently called by this *title* instead of by his name; as English people oftenest speak of their sovereign as "the Queen," instead of calling her by her name—*Victoria*.

But, as Jesus was in God's plan as the *anointed one*, before the foundation of the world, so too THE CHURCH of Christ, was recognized in the same plan; that is, God purposed to take out of the world a "little flock," whom he purposed raising above the condition of the *perfect human* nature, to make them "partakers of the *Divine nature.*" The relationship of Jesus toward these, is that of "*Head* over all, God blessed forever;" "for he hath given him to be head over *the church* (of the first-born) which is his body." As Jesus was foreordained to be *the anointed one*, so we, also, were chosen to the same anointing of the Spirit, as members in his body and under him as our head. And so we read (Eph. i, 3:) "God hath blessed us with all spiritual blessings *in Christ* according as he hath chosen us *in him* before the foundation of the world, that we should be holy and without blame before him in love; having predestinated us unto the adoption of children by Jesus Christ to himself . . . . wherein he hath made us accepted *in the beloved.*" (See also vs. 20–23.) Again, (Rom. viii, 29,) "Whom he did foreknow he also did predestinate to be conformed to the image of his Son, that he (head and body) might be the *first-born* (heir) among many brethren."

God's plan of saving *the world* by a "restitution of all things," waits until first, this bride of Jesus—these members of the Spirit-anointed body, shall be gathered out from the world according to his purpose. God's intention being to display to the world his wonderful and mighty "love wherewith he loved us," as we read (Eph. ii, 7,) "He hath raised us up together . . . . in Christ Jesus, that in the ages to come he might show the exceeding riches of his grace (favor) in his kindness toward us in Christ Jesus;" for we are "elect according to the foreknowledge of God the Father through sanctification (setting apart) of the Spirit unto obedience and sprinkling of the blood of Jesus Christ."—I Pet. i, 2. This shows us that the election is not an arbitrary one. God elected, first, that Jesus should taste death for us, thus releasing us from death; second, that the knowledge of this redemption should be declared; third, that those who believe the proclamation should be invited or called to become "partakers of the Divine nature," "heirs of God, joint heirs with Jesus Christ their Lord, if so be that they suffer (death) with him that they might be also glorified together," (Rom. viii, 17)—his purpose being, that when this "promised seed" is developed, that in, through, or by it, "all the families of the earth shall be blessed."—Gal. iii, 29. This seed is to crush the serpent's head, (Rom. xvi, 20,) thus destroying evil, and bringing about "the restitution of all things."

To be thus a part of "*The Seed*," "*The Christ*," we must see to it that we comply with the conditions, [suffer death with him if we would be found *in him*,] thus making our calling and election sure. We make sure of our being part of the elect company by obedience to the call: for, "They that are with him are called, and chosen, and faithful."—Rev. xvii, 14. Being *faithful* to the call insures our position among the chosen. "They that follow the Lamb whithersoever he goeth," in the future, are the same that bend every power and lay aside every weight to "walk in his footsteps" here.

A beautiful illustration of our oneness with Jesus, as members of his body, is shown in the anointing of Aaron as high priest. All of the anointing oil [type of the Holy Spirit] was poured upon the *head;* the under priests stood by, their heads covered with bonnets, (Lev. viii, 13,) indicating thereby that they were not the *head*. Aaron, who stood with uncovered head, was the head of their priesthood. They took part in the ceremony, and were anointed symbolically in him as members of his body, for the oil poured on the head ran down over the members of the body, as we read, (Ps. cxxxiii, 2,) "It ran down the beard, even Aaron's beard: that went down to the skirts of the garments." So we, who claim not to be the head, but members in Christ's body, receive full anointing by the same spirit. "For as the body is one, and hath many members, and all the members of that body, being many, are one body; *so also is Christ*, for by one spirit are we all baptized into one body."—I Cor. xii, 12. "As many of us as were baptized into Jesus Christ were baptized into his death."—Rom. vi, 3.

Our oneness with Jesus, as members of *the* Christ—anointed body—may be clearly illustrated by the figure of the pyramid:

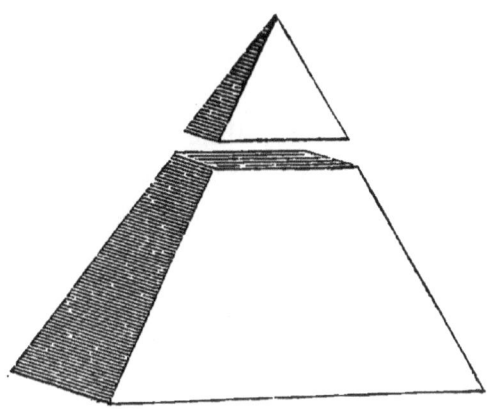

The topstone is a perfect pyramid of itself; other stones may be builded under it, and if built in exact harmony with all the characteristic lines of the topstone, the whole mass will be a perfect pyramid. How beautifully this illustrates our position as members of "The Seed"—"The Christ;" joined to, and perfectly in harmony with our head, we are perfect; separated from him, we are nothing.

Jesus, the perfect one, has been highly exalted, and now we present ourselves to him, that we may be formed and shaped according to his example, and that we may be built up as a building of God. In an ordinary building there is no "*chief* corner-stone;" but in our building there is *one* chief corner-stone, the "*topstone*," as it is written. "Behold, I lay in Zion a chief corner-stone, elect, precious"—"to whom coming as unto a living stone . . . . ye also as lively (living) stones are built up a spiritual house, an holy priesthood, to offer up spiritual sacrifices acceptable to God by Jesus Christ."—I Pet. ii, 4-6. And, very soon, we trust, the union between Jesus and the body will be complete, as expressed by the Prophet: "He shall bring forth the headstone, thereof, with shoutings of grace, grace unto it."

And, dearly beloved, many blows and much polishing must we have—much transforming we must undergo, and much conforming unto his example, under the direction of the great

Master-builder; and in order to have the ability and ideality of the builder displayed in us, we will need to see that we have no cross-grained will of ours to oppose or thwart his will being done in us; we must be very childlike and humble—"Be clothed with humility, for God resisteth the proud, but giveth grace to the humble. Humble yourselves, therefore, under the mighty hand of God, that he may exalt you in due time."—I Pet. v, 6.

PART VI.

THE PLAN OF THE AGES.

EXPLANATION OF THE CHART.

KEY.—*K*, the plane of *Glory;* *L*, the plane of *Perfect Spiritual Being;* *M*, the plane of those *Begotten of the Spirit;* *N*, the plane of *Human Perfection;* *P*, the plane of *Typical Perfection;* *R*, the plane of *Depravity and Sin*. *a*, Adam; *b*, the World; *c*, Abraham; *d*, the World; *e*, Israel; *f*, a Time of Trouble; *g*, Jesus; *h, i, k, l*, Christ Jesus; *n*, the "Little Flock;" *m*, the "Great Company;" *p*, Justified Persons; *q*, Hypocrites; *r*, Christ; *s*, the "Little Flock;" *t*, the "Great Company;" *t, u, v*, "Babylon" Falling; *S*, the "Day of the Lord" Trouble; *w, x*, Christ and Bride Enthroned; *y*, the "Great Company" before the Throne; *z*, Israel Restored; *W*, the World; *T*, the "Gate;" *U*, the "Brazen Altar;" *V*, the "Laver;" *X*, the "Golden (Incense) Altar."

IN the chart illustrative of this topic, we have sought to aid the mind through the eye, to understand something of the progressive character of God's plan; also, the progressive steps which must be taken by all who ever attain to the divine nature.

First, we have an outline of the various dispensations, *A, B, C.* The first (*A*) lasting from man's creation to the flood; the second (*B*) from the flood to the commencement of the Millennial reign at the second advent; and the third, or "Dispensation of the fullness of times," (*C*) lasting from the beginning of Christ's reign for untold ages—"ages to come."—Eph. ii, 7.

These three great dispensations are frequently referred to in Scripture: *A* being called "the world that then was;" *B* is called by Jesus "this world;" by Paul "the present evil world;" by Peter "the world that now is." *C* is called "the world to come, wherein dwelleth righteousness," thus contrasting it with the present *evil* time. Now evil rules and the righteous suffer, while in the world to come the rule is to be reversed; righteousness will rule and evil-doers will suffer, and finally all evil be destroyed, so that every knee shall bow and every tongue confess to the glory of God.

Secondly, we find that the two last of these dispensations (B and C) are composed of various ages—each of which as a successive step leads upward and onward in God's plan. Age D was the one during which God's plan was represented and typified by such patriarchs as Abraham, Isaac and Jacob, etc.

Age E is the Jewish age, or the period from the death of Jacob, during which all of his posterity are treated of God, as his especial charge—his favored people. To these he showed special favors and declared—"*You only* have I known (recognized with favor) of all the families of the earth."—Amos iii, 2. These as a nation were *typical* of the Gospel Church—the "holy nation—the peculiar people." The promises, etc., made to them were typical of "better promises" made to us. Their journey through the wilderness to the land of promise (Canaan) was typical of our journey through the wilderness of sin to the heavenly Canaan. Their sacrifices *justified them typically* and not really, "for the blood of bulls and goats .... can *never take away sin.*" But in the Gospel age (F) we have the "*better sacrifices,*" which do make atonement for the sins of the whole world. We have the "royal priesthood," of which Jesus is the chief, or "head," composed of all those who offer themselves to God "living sacrifices," holy and acceptable, through Jesus Christ. In the Gospel age we find all the *realities* of which the Jewish age and its services and ordinances were but a *shadow* —the Law being "a *shadow* of good *things* to come."—Heb. x, 1. Theirs was all *typical*, ours is all *real.*

The Gospel age (F) is the period during which the *body of Christ* is called out of the world, is shown the crown of life and the exceeding great and precious promises whereby (by obedience to the promises and high *calling*) they may become partakers of the *divine nature.*—II Pet. i, 4. Evil is still permitted to reign over or rule the world, in order that by contact with it, these may be *tried* to see whether they be willing to give up the human—a living sacrifice—being made conformable to Jesus' death, that they may be also in *his likeness* in the (*First*) resurrection. G is the Millennial age (one thousand years,) during which Christ Jesus shall reign and rule and thereby *bless* all the families of the earth, accomplishing the "restitution of all things spoken by the mouth of all the holy prophets."—Acts iii, 19–21. With this age sin and misery and death shall be forever blotted out, for "he must reign until he hath put *all enemies* under his feet . . . . The last enemy that shall be destroyed is *death*"—the Adamic death. During this reign and associated in it with Jesus, will be the church called the Bride—his body—"To him that overcometh will I grant to sit with me in my throne even as I overcame and am set down (during the Gospel age) with my Father in his throne." Blessed privilege to be thus intimately associated with our Lord in the great work of blessing all *men*—as "kings and priests unto God." *H* shows "ages to come;" ages of perfection, blessedness and happiness for all, but regarding the work of which Scripture is silent.

The "HARVEST" at the end of the Jewish age was a period of forty years, lasting from the beginning of Jesus' ministry, when he was *anointed* of God by the Spirit (Acts x, 37,) and began his ministry (A. D. 30,) until the destruction of Jerusalem (A. D. 70.) In this harvest the Jewish age ended and the Gospel age began. There was a lapping of the ages, as you will note, by careful examination of the diagram.

The Jewish age ended in a measure when, at the end of Jesus' three and one-half years' ministry, he gave them up, saying: "*Your house* is left unto you desolate."—Matth. xxiii, 38. Yet, there was *favor* shown them for three and one-half years after this by the confining to them of the *Gospel call*, in harmony with the prophet's declaration (Dan. ix, 24–27,) regarding seventy weeks (of years) of favor toward them; and "in the midst of the (seventieth) week," Messiah should be cut off (die), but not for himself ("Christ died for *our* sins:") and thus did he cause the sacrifice and oblation to cease in the midst of the week—three and one-half years before the expiration of the seventy covenant weeks. When the true sacrifice had been made, of course, the typical ones would no longer be recognized by Jehovah.

There was then a more complete sense in which that Jewish age ended with the end of the seventieth week or three and one-half years after the cross—(after which the Gospel was preached to the Gentiles also—beginning with Cornelius.)—See Acts x, 45. This ended their age so far as the *Jewish church* was concerned; but their *national* existence terminated in the great time of trouble which soon followed, resulting in the destruction of their city and nation.

In that *"harvest"* the Gospel age had its beginning also: this age is designed for the development and trial of "*the Christ of God*"—head (Jesus) and body (the church.) It is the Spirit dispensation, hence, it is proper to say that the Gospel age began with the anointing of Jesus (our head) "by the Holy Ghost, with power," (Acts x, 38: Luke iii, 22; iv, 1, 18,) at the time of his baptism; while in another sense we might say that it commenced at Pentecost, three and one-half years later, when the Spirit came upon his body, which is the church.

A "HARVEST" will constitute the closing period of the Gospel age, during which there will again be a lapping of ages—the Gospel age ending and the Restitution or Millennial age beginning. This age closes by stages, as did its pattern or "shadow" —the Jewish age. As there, the first seven years of the harvest were devoted in an especial sense to a work in and for the Jewish *church* and were years of favor; so here we find a similar seven years marked as having the same meaning and bearing upon the Gospel church, to be followed by a period of trouble (*judgments*—seven last plagues, etc., called "fire,") upon the nations of the world as a punishment for wickedness, and as a *preparation* for the reign of righteousness; of which more again.

THE PATH TO GLORY.

K, L, M, N, P, R, each represent different planes. *N* is the plane of *perfect human* nature (sinless, undefiled.) Adam was on this plane before he sinned; from the moment of disobedience he fell to the depraved or sinful plane, *R*. The world has been on that same plane since—fallen far below perfection of manhood. *P* represents the plane of *typical* justification, reckoned as effected by sacrifices of the "Law;" but it was not actual perfection, for "the Law made nothing *perfect*."

N is not only the plane of *human perfection*, as represented by the perfect man, Adam, but it is the plane occupied by all *justified persons*. "Christ died for our sins according to the Scripture," and in consequence every *believer* in Christ—all who accept of his perfect and finished work as their justifier, are, because of their *faith*, reckoned of God, justified or *perfect men* —as though they had never been sinners. In God's sight then, all *believers* in Christ's sacrifice are on the *N* plane, viz., *human perfection*. This is the only standpoint from which man may approach God, or have any communion with him. All on this plane (*N*) God calls sons (*human* sons—Adam before sin was *thus* a son, Luke iii, 38.)

During this Gospel age God has made an offer to the *justified* human beings, telling them that on certain conditions they may cease to be *earthly*, *human* beings and become heavenly spiritual beings—like unto the angels—like unto Christ's *glorious* body. Some *believers*—justified persons—are satisfied with what joy and peace they have, through believing in the forgiveness of their sins, and heed not the voice which calls them to come up higher; others moved by the love of God, as shown in their ransom from sin, say, "Lord what wilt thou have me to do?" To such the Lord answers through Paul:—"I beseech *you brethren*, by the mercies of God, that ye present your bodies a living *sacrifice;* holy, acceptable to God, your reasonable service."—Rom. xii, 1. Paul, what do you mean by our giving ourselves *living sacrifices?* I mean that you shall *consecrate* and give *every* power, which you possess, to God's service, that henceforth you shall live not for self, nor for friends, nor family, nor for the world, *nor for anything*, but for and in the service of him, who bought you with his own precious blood.

But Paul, surely God would not accept of blemished or imperfect sacrifices, and since we all became sinners through Adam, we cannot surely be sacrifices, can we? Yes, beloved, it is because you are *holy* that you are *acceptable* sacrifices, and you are holy and free from sin, because God has justified you from all sin freely through Christ's death.

As many as obey the call of Paul, rejoicing to be accounted worthy to suffer reproach for the name of Christ—those who look not at the things that are seen, but at the things that are not seen—at the "crown of life," at "the glory that shall be revealed in us," at "the prize of our high calling—in Christ Jesus"—these consecrate themselves wholly to God and are from that moment no longer reckoned *men;* but, as having been *begotten* of the Holy Ghost through the word of truth—no longer *human*, but henceforth *spiritual* children; they are now *one* step nearer the prize than when they first believed. But their spiritual being is yet *imperfect;* they are *begotten*, but not yet *born* of the spirit. They are *embryo* spiritual children on plane *M*—the plane of spiritual begetting. Because begotten of the spirit, therefore they are no longer reckoned *human*, but spiritual; for the *human nature* once theirs—once justified, they have now given up, or reckoned *dead*—a living sacrifice, holy, acceptable and *accepted* of God. They are now *new creatures* in Christ Jesus, old things (human hopes, and will and all) are passed away and all things are become new, for "ye are not in the flesh but in the spirit, if so be that the *spirit of God dwell in you*."—Rom. viii, 9. If you have been *begotten* of it, "ye are *dead* and your life is hid with Christ in God."

Plane *L* represents *perfect spiritual* being; but before plane *L* is reached, the conditions of your covenant must be carried out. It is one thing to covenant with God that you will be *dead* to all human things, and a further thing to perform that covenant throughout your earthly career,—keep your body *under* (*dead*); keep your own will out of sight, and perform only the Lord's will. The entrance upon plane *L* is called *birth*, or a full entrance into life as a *spiritual being*—like unto Christ's *glorious* body, and like unto the angels. We cannot enter on that plane until the entire church is gathered in from the world —when "the dead in Christ shall rise first," (this corruption must put on incorruption—immortality.) Then we, which are alive and remain, (not having entered the tomb) shall be changed in a moment—made perfect spiritual beings like unto Christ's glorious body (for "this mortal must put on immortality.") Then, that which is *perfect* being come, that which is in part (the *begotten* condition with the various hinderances of the flesh, to which we are now subject) shall be done away.

But there is a still further step to be taken beyond a perfection of spiritual being—viz., to "the *glory* that shall follow"—plane *K*. We do not refer to a glory of *person*, but to a glory of power or *office*. The reaching of plane *L* brings us to full *personal* glory, *i. e.*, to be *glorious beings* like unto Christ's *glorious* body. But after we are thus perfected, and made entirely like our Lord and head, we are to be associated with him in the *glory of power* and office—to sit with him in his throne, even as he after his being perfected at his resurrection, a glorious being, was exalted to the right hand of the majesty (*glory*) on high: so we shall enter in everlasting glory—plane *K*.

Now notice carefully the chart, while we look at illustrations on the path to *glory*. (A pyramid is a perfect figure or shape, hence we use it to represent perfect beings, in the chart.)

(*a*) represents Adam; he was a perfect being and hence a pyramid. Notice that he is on plane *N*, which shows that Adam was a *perfect man* (before he sinned).

Below him (*b*) is an imperfect or topless pyramid, it represents the world of mankind, which sin had degraded; notice the plane on which it stands—*R*, the "Depraved Plane."

(*c*) represents Abraham (whom we use as an illustration of several other persons.) Abraham was a member of the depraved human family, and should be on plane *R;* but Paul tells us that Abraham was *justified* by faith, that is, he was reckoned of God a (sinless) *perfect man*, because of his faith. This, in God's estimation, lifted him up above the world of depraved sinful men to plane *N;* and though *actually* still imperfect, he was received into the favor that Adam had lost, viz., *communion* with God as a "friend."—James ii, 23. All on the perfect (sinless) plane (*N*) are friends of God, and he friend of theirs; but sinners (plane *R*) are at enmity against God—"*enemies* through wicked works."

(*d*) represents the world of mankind after the flood still on plane *R*—still at *enmity*, where they continue until the Gospel church is selected and the Millennial age begins.

(*e*) represents "Israel after the flesh" during the Jewish age, when the typical sacrifices of bulls and goats cleansed them, not really, but typically; "for the *Law* made nothing *perfect.*"—Heb. vii, 19. Because they were typically justified, but not actually so, we put them on plane *P*. *The plane of typical justification*, which lasted from Mount Sinai until Jesus made an end of *the Law*, nailing it to his cross. There ended the *typical* justification by the institution of the "better sacrifices" than the Jewish types, which actually "take away the sin of the world," and "make the comers thereunto *perfect.*"

(*f*) represents the (*fire*) trial through which fleshly Israel went when Jesus was present, sifting them and taking out of their nominal church the wheat or "*Israelites indeed*, in whom was no guile," and especially after the separation of the wheat when he "burned up the chaff (refuse part of that church and nation) with unquenchable fire," (a time of trouble, etc., which they were powerless to avert.)—See Luke iii, 17; also, xxi, 22; and I Thess. ii, 16.

(*g*) represents Jesus (at thirty years of age) *a perfect man*, he having left the glory of the spiritual condition and become a *man* in order that he (by the grace of God) should taste death for *every man*. God's law requires an eye for an eye, a tooth for a tooth, and a life for a life; it was necessary that a *man* should die for mankind or the penalty (man's death) would not be paid: hence the death of an angel would no more pay the penalty and release man, than the death of "bulls and goats, which can *never take away sin*." Therefore, the first-begotten of God became a *man*, that he might give that which would redeem mankind. He must have been a *perfect* or sinless man, else he could do no more than any member of the fallen race to pay the price. He was "holy, harmless, undefiled, and *separate* from sinners." He took the same *form* or likeness which the sinners had—"the likeness of sinful flesh"—the human.

Being found in fashion as a (perfect) man, he humbled himself and became obedient unto death. He presented himself to God at baptism—"Lo I come in the volume of the book it is written of me, to do thy will, O God." When he thus presented himself—consecrated his (human) being, his offering was holy (pure) and acceptable with God, who showed his acceptance by filling him with his spirit and power—when the Holy Ghost came upon him, thus *anointing* him, thus he became the "*Christ*." [The word Christ meaning *anointed*.]

This filling with the spirit was the begetting to a higher form of being, which he should receive when he had fully accomplished the offering—sacrifice of the human nature. This was a step up from human conditions, and is shown by pyramid h, on the *spirit-begotten plane*, M. On this plane (M) Jesus spent three and a-half years of his life—until it ended on the cross. Then, after being three days dead, he was raised to life —quickened of the spirit to the perfection of *spiritual being*, (i plane L) for now he was *born* of the spirit—"The first-*born* from the dead." "That which is *born* of the spirit, is *spirit;*" Jesus, therefore, at and after his resurrection, was a spirit—a spiritual being, and no longer a human being in any sense.

True, after his resurrection he had power to, and did appear, *as a man*, in order that he might teach his disciples, and prove to them that he was no longer dead; but he was not a *man*, and no longer was controlled by human conditions, but could go and come as the wind (even when the doors were shut) and none could tell whence he came nor whither he went,—"*so* is every one that is *born* of the spirit."—John iii, 8.

From the moment of consecration (baptism) the human had been reckoned *dead*—and there the *new* nature began (begotten plane, M,) which was completed at the resurrection, when he reached the perfect spiritual plane, L—raised a spiritual body.

Forty days after his resurrection Jesus ascended to the majesty on high—the *glory plane*, K, (see pyramid k.) During the Gospel age he has been in glory, l, "set down with the Father on his throne," and during this time he has been the head over his church on earth,—her director and guide. During all this Gospel age the church is in process of development, discipline and trial to the intent, that in the end, or harvest of the Gospel age, she may become his bride and joint-heir. Hence she has fellowship in his sufferings, that she may be also glorified together with him, (plane K,) when the proper time shall come.

The steps of the church to glory are the same as those of her leader and Lord, Jesus (he hath set us an example that we should walk in his footsteps,) except that she starts for glory from a lower plane. Jesus, we have seen, came to the plane of *human perfection*, N, while all of the Adamic race are on a lower plane, R,—the plane of sin and enmity against God. The first thing then, for us to do is, to be *justified*, or get upon plane N. How is this accomplished—is it by good works? No, sinners can do no *good* works; we could not commend ourselves to God, so God commended "his love toward us (sinners, on the depraved plane, R,) in that while we were yet sinners, Christ died for us." Then the condition, upon which we come to the justified or *perfect human* plane, is that Christ *died* for our sins, redeemed us and lifted us up to the perfect plane. But, have *we* nothing to do with the matter? Nothing whatever, except to *believe it*. "We are justified (lifted to plane N) by *faith*." And "*being* justified by *faith*, we have peace with God," (Rom. v, 1,) and are no longer enemies, but justified *human sons*, on the same plane as Adam and Jesus, except that they were *actually* perfect, while we are reckoned so, of God, and *know it*, because God's word tells us so; "ye are justified freely from *all* things." We stand in God's sight absolutely spotless, because Jesus' robes of righteousness cover all our imperfections.

But remember that while *justification* is a blessed thing, it does not change your nature—you are still a *human* being, and unless you proceed you will never be a spiritual being—never be anything but a *human* being. You are saved from the wretched state of sin and alienation from God, and, instead of being a human *sinner*, you are a human son, and now because you are a son, God speaks to you as such, saying, "My son, give me thy heart:" that is, give *yourself*, all your earthly powers, will, talents—your all to me (as Jesus hath set us an example) and I will make you a son on a higher plane than the *human;* I will make you a spiritual being (*i. e.* a being with a *spiritual body*) like the *risen* Jesus—"the express image of the Father's person." If you will give up all of the earthly and consecrate it entirely to me and *use it up* in my service, I will give you a higher nature than the rest of your race—I will make you "partakers of the *divine nature*"—make you "heirs of God and joint-heirs with Christ; *if so be that you suffer with him,* that you may be also *glorified* together."—Rom. viii, 17.

Do you value this prize set before us in the Gospel? Then lay aside every weight and run with patience the race, that you may win it. Works were not called for in lifting you out of sin. No, Jesus did all the works that could be done to that end, and lifted you by *faith* to plane *N*. But now, if you would go further, you cannot go without *works*: true, you must not lose your *faith*, else you will lose your justification; but being justified you are *able* (through the grace given unto you by your begetting of the Spirit) to have *works*, to bring forth *fruit;* and God demands it. He demands that you shall show your appreciation of the grand *prize* by giving *all* that you have and are for it, not to men, but to God—a *sacrifice* holy and acceptable to him—your reasonable service. When you present all these things, say: Lord, how would you have me *deliver* these things to you? Examine the Word for God's answer and you will probably hear his voice instructing you to deliver your *all* to him as Jesus and as Paul did, viz., by "doing *good* unto all men as you have opportunity, especially to the household of faith." Serving them with spiritual or natural *food*, clothing them in Christ's righteousness or with earthly raiment, as you may have ability or they have necessity. Having consecrated *all*, you are *begotten of the spirit*—you have reached plane M, and now, through the power given unto you, if you will use it, you will be able to *do* all of your Covenant and to come off conquerors, and more than conquerors through (the power or spirit of) him who loved us and bought us with his own precious blood. Thus walking in the footsteps of Jesus—

> "Ne'er think the victory won,
> Nor once at ease sit down;
> Thine arduous work will not be done,
> Till thou hast gained thy crown."

The crown will be *won* when you, like Paul, "have fought a good fight and finished the course." You may not get the prize as soon as the race is finished and won, but may wait perhaps, as Paul did, until the entire *body* of Christ is complete, as he said: There is laid up for me a crown of righteousness which the Lord, the righteous Judge, shall give me at that day: (the day of the Lord—) and not to me only, but unto all those also who love his appearing.—II Tim. iv, 8. [We hope and *believe* that we shall not be obliged to wait in death as did Paul, but that we are living in the days of the completion of the church, which is the body of Christ, and shall be among those who shall not *sleep in death*, but be changed in a moment as Paul says: "Behold, I show you a mystery—we shall not all sleep, but we shall all be changed."—I Cor. xv, 51.]

Those of *this* class who sleep (a little flock) accounted worthy of THE resurrection (*first*) shall be raised *spiritual bodies* (vs. 44)—plane *L*. And we (of the same class—overcomers) who are alive and remain—shall be *changed*—to the same plane of being [*L*] viz., *spiritual:* like unto Christ's glorious body. No longer weak, earthly, mortal, corruptible beings, we shall *then* be fully *born* of the spirit; heavenly, spiritual, incorruptible, immortal beings. "That which is *born* of the spirit is spirit."—"I shall be satisfied when I awake in thy likeness."

We know not how long it will be after our perfecting as spiritual beings (plane *L*) before we shall be glorified (plane *K*) with him: *united* with him in power. This uniting we understand to be the "marriage of the Lamb" to his Bride, when she shall thus—enter into the joys of her Lord.

Look again at the chart—*n, m, p, q*, represent the *nominal* church as a whole, all claiming to be *the body* of Christ. *n* and *m* are both on the *spiritual begotten* plane—*M*. Both of these companies have existed throughout the Gospel age; both have covenanted with God to become living sacrifices; both have been "accepted in the beloved" and begotten of the spirit as *new creatures;* but the difference is this: *n* represents the company who are fulfilling their covenant and are *dead with Christ* to earthly will, and aims, and all. They will be the *overcomers*—the Bride—the Body who will sit with Jesus in his throne, in glory—plane *K*, when the Gospel age is ended. These are a "little flock" to whom it is the Father's good pleasure to give the *kingdom*.—Luke xii, 32. *m* represents the larger company of the spirit-begotten children; they have covenanted, but, alas! they shrink back from the performance of it —they shrink from the *death* of the human will, etc.; but God still loves them and therefore will bring them by the way of trouble and adversity—(ultimately resulting in the *destruction* of the human will)—to plane *L*—the perfect, spiritual plane. But they have lost the right to plane *K*—the throne of glory—because they were not *overcomers*. Notice that in the case of both of these companies, the earthly nature must be destroyed; but in the case of the "great company," *m*, it is taken from them, while in the case of the "*little flock*" it is, as it was, with Jesus, the example—a willing *sacrifice*. Oh, if we prize our Father's approval, if we desire our Lord's smile, if we desire to be members of his *body*—his Bride—and to sit on his throne, we must fulfill our covenant of sacrifice! I beseech you, brethren, by the mercies of God, that ye present your bodies a living sacrifice—holy, acceptable unto God, your *reasonable service*.

p represents the majority of the *nominal* church. You will notice that they are not on plane *M*, but on plane *N;* they are *justified*, but not sanctified (not entirely consecrated to God,) not *begotten*, therefore, as spiritual beings at all. They are higher than the world, because they accept of Jesus as their ransom from sin, but they have not come high enough to be a part of the *real church*—the spiritual family, and unless they progress and sacrifice the human, they will never be anything but *human*, and in the resurrection they will be in the likeness of the earthly man, Adam, whereas those who sacrifice the human, will be in the likeness of the Lord—like unto Christ's glorious body. *q* represents a class connected with the nominal church who never did *believe* in Jesus as the sacrifice for their sins and who consequently are not *justified*—not on plane *N*. They are "wolves in sheep's clothing"—they are in no sense a part of the church—they belong to plane *R*, are part of the world and are out of place in, and a great injury to, the church.

Thus, in a mixed condition, the church has existed throughout the Gospel age: as our Lord had foretold—the kingdom of heaven (church) is like unto wheat and tares in a field (the world) —"Let both grow together *until* the harvest. In the time of harvest I will say unto the reapers (the angels,) gather together the tares and bind them in bundles to burn (destroy) them, but gather the wheat into my barn.—Matt. xiii, 38, 41, 49.

These words of our Lord show us that while he purposed that both should grow together during the age, he also **purposed** that there should come a time of separating between these different elements. This *division* comes in the *end* of the age, for "the harvest *is* the end of the *age*."—Vs. 39.

During the Gospel age the seed has been growing and tares (counterfeits) also—"the good seed is the children of the kingdom"—the *spiritual* children—classes n and m—while "the *tares* are the children of the wicked one"—all of class q, and many (if not *all*) of class p—for no man can serve two masters —and "his servants you are to whom you *render service.*" As class p does not consecrate its service to the Lord, doubtless it gives much of its time and talent really in opposition to God, and hence in the service of the enemy. Now notice on the chart the "*harvest,*" or end of the Gospel age; notice the two parts into which it is divided—seven years and thirty-three years, the exact parallel of the Jewish age and harvest. This "*harvest,*" like the Jewish one, is to be a time of trial and sifting, first upon the *church*, and afterward a time of wrath or pouring out of the "seven last plagues" upon the world, and such of the church as are not separated as *wheat* during the first seven years. The Jewish harvest is the "*shadow*" or pattern on the *fleshly* plane, of all that the Gospel church enjoys on the spiritual plane. (The two cherubim which were types, also teach this equality and likeness of the two ages. They were "*of equal size and of equal measure.*")

The thing which tried (fleshly) Israel was the "stone of stumbling and rock of offence"—Jesus was present as the Lord of their harvest, (the disciples being reapers under his direction.) The truth as to *his presence* was the sickle, and it separated the "Israelites indeed in whom was no guile" from the *nominal Jewish church*, (and the *true wheat* there were but a fragment compared to the professors.) So, also, is the *harvest* of this age; Jesus comes a second time, not again a *fleshly* being, (not again to sacrifice,) but a *spiritual* body, to "*take to himself* his great power and reign"—blessing thereby all the families of the earth. (As already shown, spiritual bodies are *invisible to humanity* unless a miracle be performed.)

The second advent of Jesus, leaving the plane of glory, *K*, and coming to the unglorified spiritual plane, *L*, is shown by figure *r*. As has been stated heretofore, we believe that the prophets, etc.,* teach that we are *now* in the "*harvest*" of this age; that our Lord *has come*, and the work of harvest, or separating wheat from tares, has been progressing since A. D. 1874. The first work of the Lord in this harvest will be to separate the true from the false, and the truly *consecrated* children from the unconsecrated ones. This work we believe is now going on.

The nominal church, because of her mixed condition, the Lord calls *confusion*, or "Babylon;" and during this harvest he purposes ripening, separating, and perfecting the different classes in the church—wheat will be separated from tares, and ripe wheat from unripe, etc. Class *n* are a "first-fruits," of the wheat, and, after being separated in the spirit of their minds, will in his due time become his *Bride* and be caught away to be forever with her Lord—and like him. The separating of the little flock from Babylon is shown by figure *s*. She will ultimately become *one* with Jesus and bear his name and share his glory. The glorified Christ, head and body, is shown by figure *w*. Figures *t*, *u*, and *v* represent the "Babylon"—nominal church *falling*—going to pieces during "the time of trouble," or "day of the Lord." Though this may seem to be a dreadful thing, yet it may be shown to be of great advantage to all the *true wheat*. Babylon falls because she is *not* what she claims to be. "Babylon is fallen, is fallen, and become the habitation of devils, and the hold of every foul spirit and a cage of every unclean and hateful bird."— Rev. xviii, 2. The church nominal contains many, many hypocrites, who have associated themselves with her because of her honorable standing in the eyes of the world, who, by their conduct, etc., are gradually making Babylon a *stench* in the nostrils of the world. The Lord always knew of them, but let them alone until the *harvest*, and now will "gather out of his kingdom

---

*The chronology, time proofs, etc., can be had in a book entitled "*Day Dawn.*" Address, A. D. Jones, Pittsburgh, Pa.

(church) all things that offend and them which do iniquity, and cast them into a furnace of fire (trouble)... Then shall the righteous shine forth as the sun in the kingdom of their Father." Matt. xiii, 41. The trouble coming upon the church will, we believe, be occasioned by the overspreading of Infidelity and Spiritualism, both of which will be trials, because the church holds so many doctrines contrary to God's Word. And every one who has built his faith upon Christ with anything else than the truths of the Word—gold, silver, precious stones, will find himself sorely beset during this time of wrath (fire); for all errors of men—wood, hay, stubble—will be consumed. *s*, represents those who built with truth—gold, etc., and consequently were separated from Babylon. *t*, represents the *"great company,"* on the plane *M*—begotten of the spirit—*wheat* not fully ripened at the time of the gathering of the *first-fruits* (*s*.) They built upon the rock, *Christ Jesus*, but with wood, etc., of human creeds and isms. Such shall suffer loss (in this fire,) but himself shall be saved (so as by fire.)— I Cor.-iii, 10–15. They lose the *prize* of the throne; but, as already shown, themselves shall be saved and reach the full birth of the spirit, become spiritual beings—plane *L*. [Several Scriptures seem to teach that this company will not reach perfection on the spiritual plane *L*, until the "harvest"—and its trouble are over; while the little flock, *s*, are evidently changed before the "seven last plagues" are poured out, as they have some work to do in connection with their execution.] To return to the "great company," *t:* they were the Lord's, but they were so overcharged with the affairs of this life, the world and a worldly church, that, while the Bride was being separated from Babylon, their ears were dull of hearing; they came not out when the cry was made: The harvest is come—*"Babylon is fallen . . . . come out of her my people that ye be not partakers of her sins, and receive not of her plagues."*—Rev. xviii, 2-4; (vs. 21) And she shall be cast as a great millstone into the sea—(the world on plane *R*.) A view of this company (*t*) during the trouble, after the Bride company (*s*) has been taken and the "marriage of the Lamb is come," is furnished us in Rev. xix, 2, 5-7. It is after "Babylon" has fallen to pieces, and they are liberated from her chains and influences, and come to realize that *tares* and earthly organization never were *God's church;* but, that he always had in view the true members of Jesus body—"whose names are written in heaven." (Vs. 5), "A voice came out of the throne (*w*) saying: Praise our God all ye his servants and ye that fear him, both small and great;" then the answer of the "great company," *t* (*after* Babylon, the harlot church—church and world united, an improper union, called harlotry—has been judged, see vs. 2), saying, "Alleluia, for the Lord God omnipotent reigneth (they recognize the *reign* as commenced—by the overthrow of 'Babylon the great') let us be glad and rejoice and give honor to him, for the marriage of the Lamb is come, (Greek past tense—is accomplished) and his wife hath made herself ready." They will, no doubt, be greatly dismayed to realize that the Bride has been completed and united to the Lord, and that they, because blinded and overcharged, have lost that great prize; but seemingly (the beauty of God's plan, which they now begin to discern as one of love, both for them and for all the world of mankind, quite overcomes their grief, and they shout, Alleluia!—the glorious reign of righteousness is begun.)

Then, too, note the abundant provision of the Lord: the message is sent to them—though you are not of the Bride, you may be present at the great celebration—"Blessed is he that is called to the *marriage supper* of the Lamb," (vs. 9.) This company is called to make use of the Lord's chastisements and to come fully into harmony with him and his plan, and they shall ultimately reach the position *next to* the Bride—on the spiritual plane *L*. The time of trouble, as it will affect the world, will succeed the fall of Babylon and will be an overturning and disintegration of all human governments and of society, preparing the world for righteous and equitable government. During the time of trouble, fleshly Israel, which was cast off until the fullness of the Gentiles should be come in, will be restored to

God's favor, because the Gospel church, or spiritual Israel, will be completed. These, during the Millennial age, shall be the chief nation of earth—at the head of all on the earthly plane of being—"a praise in the whole earth."

Their restoration, as well as that of the world in general, will be a gradual one, requiring all of the Millennial age to fully accomplish it. During that thousand years' reign of Christ, death will be gradually swallowed up or destroyed. Its various stages—sickness, pain and weakness, as well as the tomb, will gradually give place before the *Great Restorer's* power, until at the end of that age the great pyramid of our chart will be complete. *x*. The Christ—the head of angels and men, next to the Father. *y*. The great company, spiritual beings, like unto the angels. *z*. Israel after the flesh at the head of earthly creatures, and *W*, the world of men restored to perfection of being like the head of the human race, Adam (before sin.) The world, as we have already seen, are to be resurrected, or again brought into existence, the penalty for their sin being paid for them in Christ's death. Their bringing again into being will be a *restoring*, and will be due during the Millennial age—the times (years) of restitution.—Acts iii, 21. It requires all of the Millennial age to accomplish the work of *restoring* to the perfection of manhood. They will then be like Adam, except that they will have enjoyed a greater range of knowledge than he possessed, both of *Good* and *Evil*. They will be mentally in the image of God; for this is a part of God's plan, that under the *new* covenant he will take away the stony heart out of their flesh, (not take away their flesh and make them spiritual beings,) and give them a heart of flesh—again as Adam's, an image of God. "This is the covenant I will make with them after those days, saith the Lord, I will put my *laws* in their hearts, and in their minds will I write them."—See Heb. x, 16; Jer. xxxi, 29; Ezek. xxxvi, 26-32. Sin is now written on the hearts of all humanity: This must first be blotted out and the former image—the law—of God reinstated before *men* will be perfect men. This work is called restitution, and this God hath promised to men. When restored they will be in no danger of falling, because no longer liable to mistake evil for good—knowing both. In Rev. xx, 9, we learn that some will be destroyed in the end of the Millennial reign, because when presented full opportunity to become perfect men, and in harmony with God and his law of *love*, they chose evil. Such die the second death, from which there is no resurrection, nor restitution. When we look at our Father's great plan for the exaltation of the church, and the blessing through her, of Israel, and all the families of the earth, by a restitution of all things, it reminds us of the song of the angels: "Glory to God in the highest; on earth peace good will toward men!" That will be the consummation of God's plan—"the gathering together of all things in (under) Christ." O the height and depth, the length and breadth, of the love of God which passeth all understanding! Who will say that God's plan has been a failure then? Who will say that he has not overruled evil for good and made both the wrath of man and of devils to praise him?

THE TABERNACLE OF THE WILDERNESS

teaches the same general lesson as the chart of the ages, and we place it alongside, that the different planes or steps to the Holy of Holies may be duly noted and appreciated. Outside the court of the tabernacle lies the whole world in sin—on the depraved plane. Entering through the "gate" into the court we become believers or *justified* persons. Those who go forward in consecration, press to the door of the tabernacle, and, entering in, become priests—are strengthened by the "shew-bread," enlightened by the candlestick, and enabled to offer acceptable sacrifices to God, by Jesus Christ, at the "Golden Altar." (Notice the corresponding planes, M and N, on the chart.) Finally, when sacrifices are all over, in the resurrection, they enter the perfect spiritual, or most holy place (plane L), and then are associated with Jesus in the glory of the kingdom. "Praise ye the Lord!"

PART VII.

THE RESURRECTION.

THE death and resurrection of a human *body* as a thing distinct and separate from the intelligent *being*, is never mentioned in the Scriptures. We never read that Abraham's *body* died, nor that Jesus' *body* died, nor that any one's *body* died.

Being signifies existence, and there can be no *being* or existence without *life and body* both. Withdraw life, and the *being* or existence ceases, for life is but a power or principle, the same in the lower animals as in man—the difference in qualities between man and the brute consisting not in a different kind of *life*, but in a different kind of *body*.

Any being is properly called a *soul* or person. This is the Scriptural sense and usage of the word *soul*, so little understood; viz., *Being* (life and body combined). Thus we read of the creation of Adam—"And the Lord God formed man of the dust of the ground and breathed into his nostrils the breath of life (*ruach*—the same breath said to be given to beasts, birds and fishes) and man became a living *soul*," (*being*.)—Gen. 2-7.

We cite a *few* illustrations out of a multitude showing the Bible usage of the word *soul*, showing that it signifies *being*. Lev. v, 2, "If a soul (*being*—person) touch any unclean thing he shall be unclean." Vs. 4, "If a *soul* (being) swear." Vs. 15, "If a soul (*being*) commit a trespass." Lev. xxii, 11, "If the priest buy any soul (*being*) with his money." Prov. vi, 7, "If he steal to satisfy his soul (*being*) when he is hungry." Jesus said, "My soul (*being*) is exceeding sorrowful even unto death." Matt. xxvi, 38, "Thou shalt love the Lord.... with all thy soul" (*being*.) Matt. xxii, 37, The rich man said, "Soul (*being*, self), thou hast much goods laid up for many years; take thine ease, eat, drink and be merry. But God said .... fool this night thy soul (*being*, existence) will (cease) be required of thee."—Luke xii, 19. "For what is a man profited if he shall gain the whole world and lose his own soul (existence, *being*,) or, What shall a man give in exchange for his soul?" (being, *existence.*)—Matt. xvi, 26. How many illustrations of this Scripture are furnished us in every-day life: Men labor for wealth, to gain as much as possible of the whole world, only to find when they are rich that wealth has come at the expense of health. How many of those who spend their life in laying up earthly treasure, find that their very *being—existence—*has been sacrificed in gaining the wealth. Then what would they not *give* to get back again health, etc.? They lavish their wealth upon physicians, traveling, etc., but it is of little use: They made a poor exchange, when they gave their being for money. Some "purified their souls (*beings* —lived more purely) in obeying the truth."—I Pet. i, 22. "The law of the Lord is perfect converting (changing) the soul"(*Being*). —Psa. xix, 7. Other souls (*beings*) were subverted, turned from the truth by error. Acts xv, 24, Other, unstable souls (*beings*, persons,) were beguiled.—II Pet. ii, 14.

With this view of the meaning of the word *soul*, viz., that it includes *all being* or existence (a combination of life and body), let us inquire—what dies—the principle of life, or the body? We answer, neither; the life principle is one which pervades all creation, just as does electricity. This principle of life prevades and is an essential element of all *being*, in tree, in fish, in fowl, in beast, in man, in angels, and in the fullest degree in God, who is its source or *fountain.* This principle cannot be said to die; though, if it be withdrawn from any creature to whom God has given it, that creature will die—cease to have *being.* Thus the breath of life is taken from beasts, birds, fish, and man.

Neither can it be properly said that the *body* dies, since, *separate from the principle of life,* the *body* never had life, and consequently could not die. The *body*, without the spirit (of life), *is dead,* and that which is dead cannot *die.*

WHAT THEN IS DEATH—WHAT DIES?

We answer, the *being* dies—ceases to have *being* or *existence.* Death is the *dissolution,* or separation of the things which, combined, constitute *being,*—namely, life and body. Thus when the spirit of life returns to God, who gave it (all nature is his reservoir of *life*), then the *being* is dead, and soon the body will return to the dust, "from whence it was taken." We see clearly, then, that not the body, but the *being*—called in Scripture *soul*— dies. Let us notice some instances in which this is stated in so many words: Job xxxi, 39, (marginal reading,) "Cause the *soul* of owners thereof to expire"—(dissolve, die.) "Their soul dieth in youth, etc." Job xxxvi, 14, margin, "To deliver their soul (*being*) from death and to keep them alive in famine."—Psa. xxxiii, 19. "He spared not their soul (*being*) from death" (dissolution.)— Psa. lxxviii, 50. He keepeth back his soul (being) from the pit" (death.)—Job xxxiii, 18. "He shall deliver his soul (*being*) from the grave."—Psa. lxxxix, 48. All souls (*beings*) are mine .... the soul (*being*) that sinneth it shall die."—Ezek. xviii, 4. It was the *soul* (*being*) of Jesus which was given for our ransom. "Thou shalt make his soul (*being*) an offering for sin" .... "He shall see of the travail of his soul and be satisfied." "He hath poured out his soul (*being*) unto death."—Isa. liii, 10-12. But, (Acts ii, 31,) "His *soul* (*being*) was not left in hell," (*hades*—the condition of death.) *He* was raised to *being* again, but a being of a higher order —having a grander than human *form* or body—"Put to death in the flesh, but quickened by the spirit." And now we come to the point—What will be *raised up*, in the resurrection? *The body*, says some one. Not so; I answer, it is the BEING that God promises to *raise up*. It once existed, and lost existence, and is to be *raised up* to existence or *being* again. Men can resurrect a body from the tomb (that is, bring a body out of a tomb to the surface); but only God's power can resurrect or *bring to existence* again a *being* who has died. We see then that resurrection means the restoring of *being*. Now, "with what body do *they* (these *beings*) come" (into being again)? is a question asked by Paul.—I Cor. xv, 35. [We have seen that *being* is made up of two elements—body, and spirit of life; hence, if restored to being, they must have some sort of bodies provided them.] Paul proceeds to tell us, that, while each must have a body, yet in the resurrection all beings will not have the *same kind* of bodies. He says that there are two general sorts or kinds of bodies—the earthly or natural bodies, and the spiritual—heavenly bodies. There are perfect illustrations of these two kinds of bodies: Adam was the head of the *earthly, human* family, and a pattern of the perfect *human being*. Christ Jesus, at his resurrection, was the first born from the dead to the perfect *new* nature, the spiritual, and he, "thus born of the spirit, is *spirit*."—John iii, 6. His is a sample or illustration of a perfect *spiritual being*.

All humanity belongs to one of two classes: either they are *natural* men—the ADAMIC SEED, or they have been begotten of the spirit through the word of truth and have given themselves up to Christ, that the will of God might be done in them; this is the *newly* begotten man; he belongs to the SPIRITUAL SEED.

Now, says Paul, "God giveth it a body as it hath pleased him and to *every seed* his own body." That is, those who have, during the present life, become partakers of the divine nature, must needs have a *divine form*—a "spiritual body," "like unto Christ's glorious body," while those who have not thus changed nature would have no change of body. When again brought into *being*, they will have natural, *human* bodies.

The resurrection, which some will have, to spiritual conditions of being—with spiritual bodies—is in Scripture designated as special, by calling it "the *first* resurrection," first in importance—*chief*. It is also frequently designated by the article THE (very noticeable in the Greek text; but less so in our English translations); for illustration—notice the following instances, (Luke xx, 35,) "They that shall be accounted worthy to obtain that world and THE resurrection neither marry nor are given in marriage." Again, Paul always taught that there would be "a resurrection, both of the just and the unjust," yet he says: If by any means I might attain unto THE resurrection.—Phil. iii, 11, (the *first*—to spiritual condition and being.) Again he designates this resurrection to spiritual being as *"his resurrection,"* because Jesus was the first one so raised to *spiritual being*. "That I might know him, and the power of HIS resurrection (*i. e.*, that I might be raised *as* he was raised). Then follows an account of *how* he might attain to that *glorious* resurrection to spiritual being, viz., "knowing the fellowship of his sufferings and being made conformable unto his death."—Phil. iii, 10.

None will attain to this *chief* resurrection, except they consecrate themselves entirely to God's service. "We beseech you therefore, brethren, by the mercies of God, that you present your bodies (and all their powers, talents, reputations—all) a *living sacrifice*, holy, acceptable unto God, your reasonable service."

So shall you be among those who shall be in THE *first* resurrection, for "blessed and holy are all they that have part in THE FIRST resurrection: on such the second death hath no power; but they shall be priests of God and of Christ, and reign with him a thousand years."—Rev. xx, 6. We can know little about the perfection, and grandeur, and powers of those who shall become spiritual beings, except that they will be "like unto Christ's *glorious* body."—Phil. iii, 21. As the apostle says: It doth not yet appear *what* we shall be, but we know that when he shall appear we shall be like him."—I John iii, 2. What an answer is this to those who claim that nothing is *real*, but a flesh-and-bone body! Who would insist that Jesus, after his resurrection, was the very same flesh and bones he was before he died? Was that a glorious body? No, that was the body he *took* for the suffering of death—but being put to death in the *flesh*, he was quickened by the spirit, "a life-giving *spirit*."—I Cor. xv, 45. Now he is the express image of the Father's person. Is the Father and Creator of all things simply a great man? Nay, verily, "God is a spirit." "It doth not yet appear, *what* . . . . but we shall be *like him*." Away with that grossness of materialism, which can realize nothing higher than the *natural*, *human* plane! Let us take Paul's account. There are human *natural* bodies and there are spiritual bodies. Both will be *glorious*, but the glory of the human, earthly, (terrestrial,) is one thing, and the glory of the spiritual, heavenly, celestial, is quite another and quite a different thing.—See I Cor. xv, 40. The restored world of mankind shall be indeed glorious *men*, like the perfect head of the human race, but that glory will not compare with "the glory that shall be revealed in us," who have given up the *human* nature and become partakers of the *divine* nature, into the perfection of which we hope soon to be ushered. Like the earthly one (Adam) *such* will they be also that are earthly (human)—Like the heavenly one, (Christ, when "born from the dead,") *such* will they be also that are heavenly (now begotten to the heavenly nature by the word of God through the spirit, then to be born into the perfection of that *being*), vs. 48.

Paul gives us a slight account of the great change from natural to spiritual, which awaits those who have part in THE *first* resurrection: Vs. 42 informs us, "Thus is THE resurrection of THE dead: It is sown in corruption, it is raised in incorruption; it is sown in dishonor, it is raised in glory; it is sown in weakness, it is raised in power; it is sown an *animal* body, it is raised a *spiritual* body." [*Diaglott.*]

ORDER IN RESURRECTION.

All of God's works and plans are full of order: It has well been said—Order is heaven's first law. While there shall be a resurrection both of the just and unjust, and *all* shall be made alive, and while some shall be made alive as perfect spiritual beings, and others in the likeness of the earthly one, Adam, yet there are times and seasons and orders for all this, as Paul says: "But every man in his *own order*, Christ the first fruits— (Jesus the *head* and we the "members of his body"—yet *"all* ONE *body"*—The head raised one thousand eight hundred years ago, the body very soon, we trust,) afterward they that are Christ's at his (*parousia*) presence—the "great company."

These are the first orders and include all of those who are of the *spiritual* family, but there are others—*every* man in his own order—and when all of these *orders are complete* (Paul mentions only those in which the church's interest centered), when all have been brought to *life* and perfection either on the human or spiritual plane (except those who die the "*second death*"), "then (at the end of the one thousand years reign of Christ and the saints) cometh the end," "when he shall have put down all rule and all authority and power." For he must reign until he hath put all enemies under his feet—"The last enemy that shall be destroyed (during that one thousand years reign) is *death*" (Adamic) in all its forms; sickness, and pain, as well as the tomb,—"Then the *end*" will have come—the *end* of sin on earth, the end of the great work of ransoming mankind and bringing them into full harmony with their Creator. Then—the Son shall deliver up the kingdom—dominion of earth to God even the Father; that God may be all—and his will done in all.—See vs. 23–28.

REVELATION XX, 5.

THE first clause of this verse, viz.—"the rest of the dead lived not again, until the thousand years were finished,"—has been the cause of much confusion and error among Christians. It is out of harmony with the teachings of both the Old and New Testaments, inasmuch as it places and fixes the resurrection of *all* except those who have part in the "*first*" (or resurrection to spiritual being) beyond and after the Millennial (one thousand years) reign of Christ and his Bride, while all other Scriptures assert that all the families of the earth are to be blessed *during* that reign; that it is for this purpose of blessing all mankind, Jesus "takes his great power and reigns;" that the period of the reign is the "Times (years) of *Restitution* spoken by the mouth of all the holy prophets," which are due to commence not at the end of the one thousand years, but at its beginning—at the second coming of Christ.—Acts iii, 19–21.

The Scripture we have just been considering (I Cor. xv, 23–28) asserts most positively that it is *during* and not after his reign (one thousand years) that Christ will put down all enemies and destroy the last enemy, *death* (Adamic). If death is destroyed during the reign, how would it be possible for any to be held by it until *after the thousand years were finished?*

Now, thank God, we can see clearly the cause of this inharmony—(probably because now is the due time—the book of Revelations has not been until recently understood). While every word of God is good, not so every word of man, and we now find that the above words of Rev. xx, 5—"The rest of the dead lived not again until the thousand years were finished"—are *man's* words and not God's.

During the "dark ages" of Papacy's reign came the "great falling away" (II Thes. ii, 3,) from about the year 300 to 1600 A. D. During that carnival of heresy several portions of the Bible were so altered as to appear to give support to Papacy's teachings—(this was in the early part of her reign, for afterward she endeavored to destroy the Scriptures under the pretence that she—the church—through her ministers was a higher authority.)

The finding in recent years of two very ancient MSS. reveals to us several interpolations of words and verses which we earnestly hope the *new version* (soon to be published) will omit, they being not God's words, but man's.

These interpolations (not *very* numerous) are of a more or less serious character, the following being probably the most important, viz., the portion of Rev. xx, 5, now under consideration; and John xxi, 25; and the words "For thine is the kingdom, the power and the glory forever. Amen"—in Matt. vi, 13; also the words "in heaven the Father, the Word and the Holy Ghost; and these three agree in one; and there are three that bear witness in earth"—parts of I John v, 7, 8.

It may not be generally known that Papacy had succeeded in destroying nearly all Greek copies of the New Testament. After "The Reformation" had made the words of Jesus and the apostles to be once more reverenced and esteemed among believers, as of greater authority than *"the voice of the church,"* our present "authorized version" (*authorized* by King James of England,) was published in the English language A. D. 1611. At the time of its arrangement and publication, but few Greek MSS. were known to exist, and only *eight* were used in the preparation of the "Latin Vulgate" from which it was translated, and none of those were older than the tenth century. Since then some six hundred and sixty MSS. have come to light, among them two very ancient ones written between the third and fourth centuries—the "Vatican MS. No. 1209," and the

"Sinaitic MS." (the latter—the very *oldest*—was found complete A. D. 1859). These MSS. are especially valuable because written before such gross errors had crept into the church and the "falling away" had reached its climax.

It is by the light shed by these ancient MSS. that we are enabled to separate between the Word of God and that of men, and to learn that the texts referred to (and some others) are *interpolations* and not a part of the *divinely inspired* Scriptures.

As to the motives and errors which may have led to these unwarranted interpolations of the text, we may be able to offer a suggestion, viz., the last mentioned (I John v, 7, 8) was probably intended to give authority and sanction to the doctrine of the "Trinity." As to the interpolation in Matt. vi, 13, and Rev. xx, 5, we may each be able to offer a reason, when it is remembered that *Papacy* claims that it is *now* the *reigning* kingdom of God—that the Millennial (one thousand years) reign of Christ and his saints over earth has been fulfilled by Papacy's reign as—Mistress of the world. As we understand it, their claim is that *since 1793 A. D.* is the "little season" in which the devil is loosed (Protestantism being his agency for *deceiving*), a fulfillment, they claim, of Rev. xx, 9.

Holding this error, is it surprising that they wanted something added to the prayer—"*Thy kingdom come*"—so as to make it appear to justify the thought that it had *already* come? This is the thought conveyed in the words *added*—"For thine *is* the kingdom, and the power, and the glory. Amen."

With this teaching, that the Papal dominion constituted the reign of Christ over the nations, yet possessing no power to resurrect the dead, is it strange that they desired to have some Scripture say that "The rest of the dead lived not again until the one thousand years were finished"? (The *first* resurrection they spiritualized.)

From our standpoint we recognize the Papal system as being the *counterfeit of the true* church which in due time shall be exalted to "power over the nations," not to bind men with chains of ignorance and superstition, but to *bless* all the families of the earth. When the true King shall—"take to himself his great *power and reign*" then we can truly say, "*Thine is the kingdom, the power, and the glory forever.*"

The words, "The rest of the dead lived not again until the thousand years were finished"—are not found in any MSS. written previous to the *fifth* century, and if we notice the connections in which they are found, we will see that they are as much out of harmony there as we have just seen it to be incongruous with the general teachings of other parts of the Bible. The succeeding clause of the same verse is by this interpolation forced to say that "*this* (after the one thousand years) is the *first* resurrection." Now read verses 4-6, omitting the interpolated clause, and we have harmony and sense—"They lived and reigned with Christ a thousand years: *This* is *the first* resurrection; on such the second death hath no power, but they shall be priests of God and of Christ and shall reign *with him* a thousand years."

PART VIII.

THE NARROW WAY TO LIFE.

"Enter ye in at the strait gate, because strait is the gate and narrow is the way that leadeth unto *life*, and few there be that find it; for wide is the gate and broad is the way that leadeth to destruction, and many there be which go in thereat."—Matt. vii, 14.

ALL life is the same. It all issues from the same fountain. God is that fountain. In him, and in him only, is life unlimited, exhaustless, ever-continuous and uncontrolled by any circumstances. The name, which describes this perfection of life, is *Immortality*. It signifies death-proof, consequently *disease and pain-proof*. Many, who have not closely noted the scriptural use of the word immortal, have used it with reference to man and to angels, but Scripture ascribes it to *God, the Father, only*, as we will prove shortly.

The sun is the great fountain of light to earth, illuminating all things, yet it causes many varieties of color and shades of light, according to the nature of the object upon which it shines. The same sunlight shining upon a diamond, a brick, and upon various kinds of glass, produces strikingly different effects. The light is the same, but the objects upon which it shines differ in their capacity to receive and transmit it. So, too, with life. It all flows from the one inexhaustible fountain, and is all of the same kind. The oyster has *life*, but its organism is such that it cannot make use of much life, just as the brick cannot reflect much of the light of the sun. So with each of the higher grades of life in beast, fish and fowl. Like the various kinds of glass under sunlight, so these various creatures show forth differently the various qualities and powers they possess, when life comes in and animates their bodily powers. And as the diamond is so perfect in its nature, and so adapted that it can receive fully and reflect, so as to look as though it possessed within itself the light, and were itself a miniature sun, so with mankind, one of the master-pieces of God's creation, made only "a little lower than the angels." This perfect creature was made so complete in his organism (before sin marred it) as to be able to receive and retain life, and never grow dim. Adam was formed grandly and perfectly, and filled with life. He was more grand than any other earthly creature, because of the grander organism, mental and physical. Yet let us remember, that, as the diamond could reflect no light, except when shone upon by the sun, so man could possess and enjoy the life given him only so long as he was supplied from the fountain—God. Man is no more a fount of life than a diamond is a fount of light, and one of the very strongest reasons for knowing that we have no exhaustless supply of life in ourselves is, that since sin entered, our race has lost life. Millions have gone and are going down into death. God had arranged that man should have access to life-giving trees, and that, by continually partaking of their fruit, he should continually live,—"eat, and live forever."—Gen. iii, 22.

Sin entering, our race lost its right to life, and was shut away from the trees of life (plural). And the glory and beauty of humanity is dependent on the supply of life, just as the beauty of the diamond is dependent on the supply of sunlight. When sin deprived humanity of the right to life and its supply was withheld, immediately the jewel began to lose its perfection of brilliancy and beauty, and finally it is deprived of its last vestige in the tomb. "His beauty consumes away like a moth."—Psa. xxxix, 11. And so "In Adam all die." But God has provided Christ a ransom for sin, and soon in [by] Christ shall all be made alive—be brought back to the *original perfection* of the race. As the diamond loses its beauty and brilliancy when the light is withdrawn, but is lighted up again with the sunrise, so mankind loses life when God withdraws life from him. "Yea, man giveth up the ghost [life], and where is he?"—Job. xiv, 10. "His sons come to honor, and he knoweth it not, and they are brought low, but he perceiveth it not of them."—Vs. 21. "For there is no work, nor device, nor knowledge, nor wisdom, in the grave whither thou goest."—Eccl. ix, 10. But the jewel is to have its beauty restored, and is again to reflect perfectly the Creator's image, "when the sun of righteousness shall arise with healing in his wings." Because of the sin-offering and sacrifice of Christ, all shall go forth from this condition of death. "All that are in their graves shall come forth." There shall be a restitution of all things, a restoring to the condition (as at first) when man can receive back again, and richly enjoy *life* as it is provided for him in *full measure* from the fountain—God.

But we asserted that we would prove scripturally that divinity is the only fountain of life, and that all other forms of life—angels, men, fish, birds, beasts, etc.,—are only vessels which hold each its full, all differing in capacity and quality, according to the will of the Maker. First, then, we read that God "*only* hath immortality." [The fulness of *life* which could not cease under any circumstances.]—I Tim. vi, 16; and i, 17. "Who *only* hath immortality, dwelling in the light which no man can approach unto; whom no man hath seen, nor can see." "Unto the king eternal, *immortal*, invisible, the only wise God, be honor and glory for ever and ever."

Secondly, we learn that the Father, who alone possessed this quality originally, has bestowed it upon our Lord Jesus Christ —his son—"the first-born of every creature;" "the only begotten;" "the express image of his Father's person;" he who was "made so much better than the angels;" "for unto which of the angels said he [the Father]: Thou art my son; this day have I begotten thee."—Heb. i, 4, 5. This one, we are told, partakes of the Father's nature, and consequently of the same principle of *immortal life*. So we read—"As the Father hath *life in himself*, [God's life is *in* himself, and not drawn from other sources, or dependent upon other things,] so hath he given to the Son to have *life in himself.*"—John v, 26.

Thus we see that immortality is possessed only by Father and Son. But amazing news!—God purposes to call out of the human race a few, a "little flock," who by obedience to certain *conditions*, shall become "sons of God," and these, instead of continuing to be of the human nature—men—shall become "*new creatures*;" "partakers of the *divine* nature." These, when born from the dead in the resurrection (as Jesus was) will have the divine form (body), being made "like unto Christ's glorious body;" (and he is "the express image of the Father," as above quoted) not a *natural* body, but a *spiritual body*, for "it is raised a spiritual body," and "that which is born of the spirit is *spirit.*" We shall be changed, but "it doth not yet appear what we shall be, but we know that when he shall appear, we shall be *like him*" who is "the express image of the Father's person," and share in the "glory to be revealed." Nay, more, not only will these be in the divine form and nature, but being of that nature, they will possess the same perfection of life—*Immortality*. Hence we read: "And this is the record that God hath given unto us eternal life, and this life is *in his Son*"—"He that hath the Son *hath life;* he that hath not the Son *hath not life*" (*immortal*).—I Jno. v, 11.

Again it is written: "Thou hast given him (Jesus) power over all flesh, that he should *give eternal life* to as many as thou (the Father) hast given him.—Jno. xvii, 2. "And this is the promise which he hath promised us, even *eternal life*."—I Jno. ii, 25. And though it is promised as a gift, yet it is only to a certain class that he ever agreed to give it, viz., to those believers in Jesus who by patient continuance in well-doing SEEK for *glory*, *honor* and IMMORTALITY."—Rom. ii, 7. To those who flee from iniquity and "follow after righteousness, godliness, faith, love, patience, meekness"—who "fight the good fight of faith (and thus), lay hold on *eternal life*, whereunto thou art also *called*." —I Tim. vi, 12.

But the way is a difficult one, hard to walk in. Just how difficult the way is, may be judged from Jesus' words: "Strait is the gate and narrow is the way that leadeth unto *life*, and few there be that find it" (*life*). It is not only to believe on him, but to follow him, and obey his voice—"My sheep hear (obey) my voice and I know them and they follow me, ("take up their cross and follow me,") and I give unto *them eternal life*." Jno. x, 28. Yes, dearly beloved, if we would be of those who receive immortality, let us *seek* it earnestly. Let us have our "fruit unto holiness (entire consecration) and the end thereof (will be) *everlasting life*."—Rom. vi, 22.

The new, divine nature begins with us here, when, after belief on Jesus as the ransom from sin, we covenant with God that we will "*die with him* that we may also *live with him*." From that moment we are recognized as God's children, and "he sends forth his spirit into our hearts," "whereby (we) are sealed (marked off as separate from the world) unto the day of redemption." This is our new life begun. By this new life we are to crucify the old will—our will as *natural* men—and while in the world "to live according to God in the spirit." The spirit in us is the *germ* of immortality. Thus we even now are partakers of the divine nature, but the fullness is to be reached when we enter into life. We are *now begotten* of the spirit by the word of truth that we should be a kind of first fruits, but we do not reach *birth* until we are raised (from the dead) spiritual bodies. Our new nature lives in these mortal bodies as in a house—"But we know that if our earthly house of this (building) were dissolved, we have a building of God," etc.—our *spiritual, immortal* condition.

But, beloved, the new life would be easily choked, and Paul assures us that when thus begotten of the spirit through the truth, "if we live after the flesh we shall die (lose our life principle), but if we through the spirit do mortify (put to death) the deeds of the body (human nature) we (as *new* creatures) shall live;" for the sons of God are all those led by the spirit of God.—Rom. viii, 13, 14. The work of crucifying must take hold upon all our actions—"For he (begotten of the spirit) that soweth to the flesh (lives in wilful sin) shall of the flesh reap corruption; but he that soweth to the spirit shall of the spirit reap *life everlasting*."—Gal. vi, 8. It is a rugged, steep, narrow way that leads to life, and were it not that strength is furnished us for each successive step of the journey, we never could reach the goal; but our Captain's word encourages us—"Be of good cheer, *I have overcome*," "*my grace* is sufficient *for thee*." The whole race was in the broad road and going down to destruction —death—until Jesus opened the narrow way, bringing life and immortality to light through the Gospel; *i. e.*, he made it possible for us to reach it, by paying our ransom on the cross and making us free from sin, and becoming also our example and leader into the divine *life*.

Thus he opened up for us a new and living way through the vail, that is to say, his flesh.—Heb. x, 20. As we have seen, we were created on the perfect natural plane (represented in Adam) and no higher hope than that of being natural men was ever held out, until Jesus paid our ransom price—that is to say, his flesh, and opened up this new way (though a narrow, difficult one) by which believers could go beyond the vail—beyond the natural condition into the spiritual. ["For the things that are seen are temporal—natural—but the things that are not seen are eternal."—II Cor. iv, 18.]

We can hardly impress too strongly the fact that all of the promises ever held out to the Jews, during previous ages, were only such as pertain to the natural man—*i. e.*, natural life, prosperity and blessing. The first offer of anything spiritual was made by Jesus to those who believe on him during this Gospel age. These are promised, that in the resurrection they shall be spiritual bodies—"That which is *born* of the spirit is spirit." But notice that though this promise of spiritual instead of human existence is to *all* believers, yet there is a still higher promise made to some of the believers, viz., *Immortality*. There is a vast difference between everlasting life and immortal life; the first signifies an ever-continued existence, which may be dependent on circumstances, as for instance, angels and men. Adam, if he had kept his first estate of sinless perfection, would have "lived forever;" and angels, though of a higher nature than human, have *life* continued to them on the same conditions of *obedience;* and some of them, "those angels who kept not their first estate" of purity and sinlessness ("the devil and his angels") are to be destroyed—have *life* taken from them.

It will be seen then, that *ever*lasting life may be enjoyed by creatures of God on either the natural or the spiritual plane, and that the condition upon which it may be enjoyed is *everlasting obedience* to the author and fountain of life—God.

This everlasting life is guaranteed to all creatures who use their life in harmony with God's will. It was on this account the world needed both, a Redeemer to pay for them the price of sin—death, and a Restorer to bring them again to the condition of perfection enjoyed by Adam, in which it was possible to render perfect obedience to God's will; which ability to obey was lost through sin.

Now let us notice the difference between everlasting life and immortal life. Immortal life is everlasting, but it is more: it is a life which cannot cease under any conditions; a life power inherent in the being possessing it, not supplied by food or other conditions, as is all other life, both of angels and men. "Man did eat *angel's food.*"—Psa. lxxviii, 25.—"Of every tree of the garden thou mayest freely eat."—Gen. ii, 16.) In a word, as already scripturally expressed, it is to have "life *in* himself," to be a fountain of life—a means of supplying life to others.

With this, which we believe to be a scriptural definition of immortality, who for a moment would wonder that it was originally possessed only by God the Father—"the King eternal, invisible, the only wise God," "who only hath immortality?" (I Tim. i, 17, and vi, 16,) or that in due time it was bestowed upon our Lord Jesus, as we read—"As the Father hath *life in himself*, (immortal,) so hath he *given* unto the Son, that he should have *life in himself.*" Jesus, before he "took the form (nature and life) of a servant," and "was found in fashion as a man," was, we understand the Scriptures to teach, a spiritual being—*i. e.*, a spiritual, and not a human body. He was the chiefest of all God's creatures—"the beginning of the creation of God."—Rev. iii, 14. Yet, to our understanding, he did not, at that time, possess *immortality;* though, like angels and all intelligent beings living in obedience to the Creator, he was guaranteed *everlasting* life as long as obedient.

This life, which, according to God's plan, he had a right to possess, he desired to give as a ransom for ours. But how should he do it? If he *died, a spiritual being*, it would have done us *human beings* no good whatever. It was a human, and not a spiritual being, which was condemned to death, and God's law of "an eye for an eye" and a "life for a life," demanded a human sacrifice for human sinners. Nay; had *ten thousand* spiritual beings died, that could never have redeemed mankind, any more than could ten thousand "bulls and goats, which can never take away sin."—Heb. x, 4. Neither a higher nor a lower order of beings could redeem; it required *a man* to redeem mankind. Therefore, this spiritual being changed his condition of existence from the spiritual to the human, and on earth was known as Jesus. It was *not a death* of the spiritual being, but a *transferrence of life* from a higher to a lower plane of existence—the perfect plane of being, which Adam had forfeited by sin.*

The penalty of Adam's sin was death (everlasting,) and when Jesus took his place he became subject to that penalty—eternal death. Jesus, as *a man*, then, in order to redeem man must give up forever his human existence. This giving up was at the time of his baptism, and his death was typified in that act. But after *giving up*, or consecrating his life as a ransom, he was three and a half years in actually *giving it up*—spending it in the service of others and finally ending it on the cross. When he consecrated himself unto death (at baptism), he received his *begetting* of the spirit to the new life—the divine, immortal life; and at his resurrection he was born to that new nature and life, a spiritual body, and never again took the human, which he had given as "*a ransom* for many." In all of this he is the pattern, or leader of all the "little flock," who consecrate and sacrifice the human, and "become partakers of the divine nature."

Thus "Christ died for our sins according to the Scriptures"— "A body hast thou prepared me for the suffering of death," etc., "and being found in fashion as a man, he humbled himself unto death, even the death of the cross." Thus he died as *a man* for mankind, or as Paul expresses it: "Since by *man* came death, by *man* came also the resurrection of the dead."—I Cor. xv, 21. He died the just [man] for the unjust [men] that he might bring us to God.—I Pet. iii, 18. We next notice, that the *thing* given for the life of the world, was the life of Jesus (the man): "For

---

* Such a transferrence, or change of life, from one condition to another, will occur, when "we, who are alive and remain, shall be caught up to meet the Lord," "changed in a moment" from human to spiritual conditions without tasting death. In Jesus' case the life was *transferred* from a higher to a lower plane of being; in our case, it will be from the lower to the higher. Our life will be swallowed up of *immortality*, or perfection of life.

the Son of Man came .... to give his *life* a ransom for many" [lives].—Mark x, 45. Notice again that the life Jesus gave was *all* the life he possessed—it was *his life*. In the parable of the treasure hid in the field, (Matt. xiii, 44.) "the Kingdom of Heaven is likened unto a treasure hid in a field ['the field is the world' of mankind—the bride of Christ, the hidden treasure,] which, when a man [Jesus] hath found, he goeth and *selleth all that he hath* and buyeth that field." Jesus gave his *all* and so must those who would be joint-heirs with him, walk in his footsteps and sacrifice earthly life.

Now, as an immortal being *cannot* die, it seems clear that Jesus did not have immortality when he died. It would be impossible for an immortal being to suffer pain or to die. But Jesus assures us that "the Father hath *given* unto the Son that he should have life in himself."* When was it *given* unto him? Paul tells us it was after he died,—at his resurrection. Hear him: "Christ Jesus, who being in the form of God [a spiritual being] thought it not robbery to be equal with God; [to speak of himself as being a member of God's family—the *Son* of God"— John x, 35, 36] but made himself of no reputation, and took upon him the form of a servant, and was made in the likeness of men. And being found in fashion as a man, he humbled himself and became obedient unto death, even the death of the cross. "WHEREFORE, [because of this obedience—death on the cross, etc.] God also hath *highly exalted him, and given him a name*, which is above every name, that at the name of Jesus every knee should bow, both of things in heaven and things in earth, and things under the earth, ['they that are in their graves'—the dead], and that every tongue should confess that Jesus Christ is *Lord* to the glory of God the Father."—Phil. ii, 6-11. "That all men might honor the Son, even as they honor the Father."— Jno. v, 23.

From this and other Scriptures it seems evident, that, while Jesus had held a very high position in the spirit world before taking the human nature and form, yet the position occupied by him since he ascended up on high, is a much higher one—" Him hath God highly exalted," etc.,—and the word *wherefore*, (on this account) used by Paul, clearly shows that the high exaltation came as a reward for the self-sacrifice and obedience even unto

---

* Jesus, after he had consecrated himself and had been begotten of the new, divine nature, spoke of the new life which was promised him, and which he received fully at the resurrection as though he had already received it; just as it is said of us—" He that believeth .... *hath* everlasting life."

death. This high exaltation consisted in part of the glory of power, which will be fully displayed and exercised during the Millennial age. But who can doubt that one of the chief elements of that high exaltation was *immortality*, heretofore possessed only by "the King of kings and Lord of lords, the only wise God?"

This mighty one—Jehovah—received our Lord, the perfect one, whose life and death were one grand expression of love to God and to men, into *oneness of life*, as well as of glory and power with himself, which would imply his becoming the son of God with power, (in a higher sense than before) and a partaker of the *divine* nature. How fitting, too, that he, whose work it is to *restore* the human race again to perfection of earthly being, should be a *fountain of life!*

Every action should have a motive; and when Jesus came into the world and died for our sins, it was the result of one or more motives. And so we find Paul, in exhorting the church to a life of self-sacrifice, pointing to the prize of our high calling as a motive or incentive to energy and perseverance; and he refers to Jesus as our example, saying: "Consider him that endured—... looking unto Jesus, the author and finisher of our faith; who, *for the joy set before him*, endured the cross, despising the shame, and is set down at the right hand of the throne of God."—Heb. xii, 2, 3.

The joy set before our Lord was threefold: first, to ransom a race of beings from sin and death, and restore them to the perfection of their being; second, as a reward for his faith in God's promise, and obedience to his will, *he* would be exalted to the right hand (chief place) of power, and have inherent life ("life in himself,") the divine degree—immortality; third, he might bring *some* of the human race to the higher plane of being —the spiritual. To these he would be both redeemer from death and leader—to as many as believed on him, "to them gave he *power to become* the sons of God."—John i, 12. These could also become partakers of the divine nature (II Pet. i, 4), be associated with him as his Bride—become heirs of God, and *joint*-heirs with himself.—Rom. viii, 17. But how should these ever be counted worthy of exaltation to such a position of glory and honor, side-by-side with him who is the express image of the Father's person? By following in his footsteps: he became the leader of a "little flock" of believers, who, after being redeemed by his sacrifice, should, by following his example— giving up the human life, will, ambition, etc., and walking after the law of the spirit, be counted worthy to become his *Bride*. These suffer with him, that they also may be glorified together (with him.)—Rom. viii, 17. Yes, this was a part of his mission, and therefore a part of his joy—to bring up some of the human family to the *divine* nature. So we read: " It became him (God) for whom are all things, and by whom are all things, in bringing many sons unto glory, to make the captain of their salvation (Jesus) perfect through suffering."—Heb. ii, 10. Jesus must go through the most severe trials to prove his obedience to the Father's will before being entrusted with the high honor of *glory* and *immortality*. And he came off victor—proved his perfection by *obedience* even unto death. He was tried and not found wanting; "tried in all points, like as we are, yet *without sin;*" he won the "prize of his high calling—the joy set before him."

At the resurrection of Jesus we reach a point of time where *two* beings possess the principle of immortality—the Father and the Son. Now we learn that this principle of immortality is promised also to the *Bride* of Christ. Who then will constitute the Bride? Jesus tells us, "many are called and few are chosen." Paul estimates that many run, though few *so run* as to obtain the prize of the high calling; yet Jesus assures the little flock who do *so* run that "it is the Father's good pleasure to give [them] the kingdom." Not all believers then, nor even the majority, but a "little flock" who *overcome* the world, will constitute the Bride—the Lamb's wife—"To him that overcometh will I grant to sit with me in my throne."—Rev. iii, 21.

We have already seen that the Gospel church, when fully developed, will be composed of two classes. These two classes will embrace all who have believed in Jesus as the sin-bearer, and have consecrated themselves to his service—all who, during the Gospel age, have been begotten to a newness of life by the spirit through the Word, except a very few mentioned by Jesus, John and Paul as those who sin against the Holy Ghost, which sin hath never forgiveness. Paul, in Heb. vi, 4-6, describes those committing this sin as having been once enlightened and having tasted of the heavenly gift and of the good word of God, and the powers of the world to come, and being made partakers of the Holy Ghost, (*i. e.*, begotten by the holy spirit); nevertheless they crucify to themselves the Son of God afresh and put him to an open shame . . . . (Heb. x, 29) counting the blood of the covenant, wherewith they were sanctified an unholy thing, and doing despite unto the spirit of grace. In a word, these are open, *wilful apostates* (not weak, backsliding Christians, whose love is chilled for a time by contact with the cold world.) These apostates will die the second death, but all others of the church being begotten of the spirit, will in due time, at the resurrection be born of the spirit to spiritual conditions—spiritual bodies. But many, though believers, have not continued to grow up into Christ, but have remained children, consequently were too weak to overcome the world. They are bound by the world's customs, business, money-making, pleasures of this life, honor of this world, etc., and do not follow the "Captain of their salvation" in the "narrow way," and such must have much scourging and discipline before the fleshly nature is subdued; such must go through a time of trouble—be "delivered over to Satan [evil] for the *destruction* of the flesh, that the spirit [new nature] may be saved in the day of the Lord Jesus."

This class constitute the majority of all the Christian church—the "*great company*" who come up [to the spiritual condition] out of [through] great tribulation and wash their robes and make them white in the blood of the Lamb."—Rev. vii, 14. The *few*, the "little flock" will win the prize for which all are called to run. The prize of our high calling is, to become "heirs of God, joint-heirs with Jesus Christ our Lord," or as again expressed: We "seek for glory, honor and immortality."—Rom. ii, 7. If you would realize its grandeur, think for a moment that this is the same prize for which Jesus ran; the same joy that was set before him—*Glory, Honor, and Immortality*. He has been exalted, and now of the many called to share with him, in the honor and glory of his exalted position, the few who will be chosen, are making their calling and election sure by walking in "the narrow way"—"the way their leader trod." And we repeat, only the few win that prize for which all seek—glory, honor and immortality. "If we be *dead* with him [to the fleshly nature] we shall also live with him."—Rom. vi, 8. As Jesus said: "To him that overcometh will I grant to sit with me in my throne, even as I also overcame and am set down with my Father in his throne."—Rev. iii, 21.

These *overcomers* who worship not the symbolic beast or image (Rev. xx, 4) constitute the first resurrection, of which Jesus was the first-fruits: "Blessed and holy is he that hath part in the first resurrection; on such the second death hath *no power* [because they are immortal], and they shall be priests of God and of Christ and shall reign with him a thousand years."—Rev. xx, 6.

Here, then, are the conditions upon which we may attain to

the highest position in the gift of God. Nor should we be surprised that the way that leads to life is narrow, when we realize the grandeur of the life to which it leads. The masses of the church, as we have seen, walk not in the *narrow way* and consequently do not receive the prize of our high calling. Though begotten of the spirit, they try to walk upon a middle road; they try to keep both the favor of God and the favor of the world, forgetting that "the friendship of the world is enmity against God," and that the instructions to those running the race for the prize are "Love not the world," "Seek not honor one of another, but that which cometh of God only."

These, who, as we have seen, "love the present world," receive a scourging and purifying by fire of trouble, and are finally received into the heavenly—spiritual condition. They will have everlasting life as angels have it, but will lose the prize of *Immortality*. These shall serve God in his temple, and stand *before* the throne, having palms in their hands (Rev. vii, 9-17); but though that will be glorious, it will not be so glorious as the position of the "little flock" who shall be kings and priests unto God, seated with Jesus in his throne as his bride and joint heir, and with him crowned with *Immortal*, divine life.

The balance of our race now thronging the broad road to death are to be *restored* because their guilt and sin are atoned for and will be remitted. As through the disobedience of one man all were placed upon the broad road and swallowed up of death, so, through the obedience of one (Christ), all will be forgiven and brought back to life. But when brought back to "*their former estate*"—the perfection of the original—they will not have life in the same sense that the Divine family will have it. Theirs will not be life in themselves, but supplied life. The restored race will, no doubt, *live eternally*. God will supply the means of continuing their life as long as they are obedient, and that, we are told, will be forever. Doubtless their present experiences with sin will prove a blessing throughout eternity.

The words Incorruptible, Incorruption, Immortal, and Immortality are translations of the Greek words *athanasia, aphtharsia*, and *aphthartos*. (These words have the same significance, viz., "Incapable of corruption—decay—death." "Having unlimited existence."—Webster.) These occur in all only eighteen times, in Scripture and are always used in connection with God or the saints, and are never associated in any way with angels, mankind, or lower orders of creation.

With a glimpse of this "*crown of life* which fadeth not away" and the honor and glory associated with it, who will say that our all-wise Father has made the pathway too difficult? Its difficulties will act as a separating principle to separate and refine a "peculiar people," "a little flock," to be "heirs of the kingdom," "heirs of glory," heirs of God and joint heirs with Jesus Christ our Lord—if so be that we suffer (death) with him.

As we toil upward on the *narrow way*, angels look on amazed at the grandeur of the plan which is able not only to rescue a fallen race from death, but to display "the *exceeding riches* of God's grace and loving-kindness towards us who are in Christ Jesus."—Eph. ii, 7. And it will yet be more clearly seen in the ages to come. Yes, when the plan was first foretold through the prophets, angels desired to look into it and to know concerning the time, and manner of time of its fulfillment (see I Peter i, 12), and an "innumerable company of angels" still watch our progress and gladly become "ministering spirits," "sent forth to minister for those who shall be heirs of salvation" (Heb. i, 14), and soon be their rulers: for, "know ye not that ye shall judge (govern) angels?"—I Cor. vi, 3. The Father, too, who has called us with so high a calling, looks upon us with loving sympathy, and desires that we make our calling and election sure by complying with the conditions. And there is another who watches us with intense interest: it is he who redeemed us from death by his own precious blood and invited us to become his Bride and joint heir. If he loved us with such love while we were yet sinners, judge of his love now that we are his betrothed. He knows all about the *narrow way*—was tempted in all points as we are, without yielding, and now he stands ready to succor and strengthen us as we need and ask his help.

In view of all these things, let us, brethren and sisters, "come boldly unto the Throne of Grace, that we may obtain mercy and find grace to help in every time of need," while we fight the good fight of faith (warfare of the new against the old nature) and lay hold on *eternal life*.

THE BROAD ROAD TO DESTRUCTION.

THE road is so steep that when once we are fully started upon it, it seems almost impossible to avoid running headlong to its end. Six thousand years ago, Adam, (and we in him as a race of human beings,) was driven from the garden of Eden, because of sin, and sentenced to *destruction;* God's law being that any creature who will not live in harmony with his law shall *not live at all*. "The soul (*being*) that sinneth, it shall *die*."—Ezek. xviii, 4. Thus God drove us out from the life-giving trees of Eden, saying: "Dying thou shalt die." And as a sinner condemned to destruction, our father Adam started forth upon the "*broad road*" which leads to it. Slowly he walked in that way; he hasted not to its end for nine hundred and thirty years. As years rolled on, and the path became more and more smoothly worn, the race sped more rapidly to destruction. The way becomes daily more glazed and slimed and slippery with sin, and the various appliances for hastening men to death, in use by "him that has the power of death, that is, the devil."—Heb. ii, 14. And not only is the way more slippery, but mankind daily loses the power of resistance, so that now the average length of human life is about thirty years. We get to the end of this broad road nine hundred years quicker than did the perfect man. In fact, so weak and degraded has our race become, that its condition is painfully described as "prone to sin as the sparks to fly upward." So, then, as we look about us, we can pity, as well as abhor, the murderer, the licentiate, the thief, the liar, and the drunkard. We abhor the sins, but we pity the poor fellow-being so degraded as to be under their control, and God loves and pities them too; and hence he has made provision (as other Scriptures have shown us) whereby Christ died for and redeemed all on this broad road, and in due time will restore them to their first (Adamic) estate. But let *us*, if we see the "*narrow way*," walk in it, and thus be prepared and permitted to share in the work of restoring all things.

PART IX.

THE THREE GREAT COVENANTS.

A COVENANT is an agreement. God, who knows the end from the beginning, never made a covenant which he could not and will not fulfill. Covenants may be conditional or unconditional: where a *conditional* covenant was made, *i. e.*, where each party to it was bound to do certain things, it was customary to appoint a *mediator*—a person who stands between and whose business it is to see that both parties keep their covenant. God has made several covenants, but *three in particular*, which we wish now to consider briefly. These are, first, the "covenant with Abraham;" second, the covenant of "the Law;" third, the "New covenant."

The first one reads: "In thee and in thy seed shall all the families of the earth be blessed." This covenant we understand to cover *two* classes—Abraham and his seed through Isaac, and he whom Abraham typified—Jehovah and his seed through Jesus. The blessing comes first through the *God-seed*—Christ and his brethren, the church, reaching, blessing and *restoring* the fleshly seed first, and through them extending to and blessing all the families of the earth. Thus we see *how* the blessing will "be sure unto *all* the seed."—Rom. iv, 16. Now, we inquire, are there any conditions to this first covenant? If there are—it is possible that Abraham and his seed might fail to keep their part and so the conditions and covenant being broken, God *may never fulfill* that covenant. But, we answer, there were *no conditions.* God did not say, Abraham, *if* you and your seed after you will obey me, I will do thus and so, but he simply tells Abraham what he intends doing. That covenant then cannot pass away, nor be altered, nor added to,—(Gal. iii, 15, 17,)—it must be fulfilled just as it reads. The seed *must* come and the seed *shall bless all* the families of the earth. How much this is in harmony with the teaching of a "restitution of all things!"—Acts iii, 21. If further evidence that this first covenant was *unconditional* be desired, it is found in the fact that no mediator was appointed; none was needed since there was only *one* party

(God) who covenanted anything—Gal. iii, 20. That covenant was confirmed by an oath.—Heb. vi, 13-18. The second covenant we wish to consider is "the Law." It was delivered to Israel at Mount Sinai. Unlike the first, it had conditions—if Israel would obey *the Law*, they should be "a peculiar treasure above all people:" for, says God, "all the earth is mine, and ye shall be a kingdom of priests and an holy nation."—Exod. xix, 5. Then follows the words of their covenant.—Exod. 20 to 23. Moses declares, (in harmony with Gal. iii, 17,) "The Lord made not *this* covenant with our fathers [Abraham, etc.] but with us, even us who are all here alive this day. The Lord talked with you face to face in the mount out of the midst of the fire, and *I stood between the Lord and you* at that time."—Deut. v, 2-5.

The whole world were sinners but knew not to what extent; they knew not that they were so depraved that they could not keep God's law perfectly. And it was God's object in making the Law Covenant, to prove to Israel their own *imperfection* and inability to live in harmony with God. Therefore he said to them, after making the conditions of the covenant and when the people had accepted it, "Ye shall therefore keep my statutes and my judgments *which if a man do* he shall *live*."—Lev. xviii, 5; see also Rom. x, 5, and vii, 7, 12, 13, 16.

Therefore, when God made this second covenant, he knew that Israel would never realize the promises therein given, because they would not be able to keep it—all being sinners—for "by the deeds of the Law shall no flesh be justified." "That *no man* is justified by the Law is evident."—Gal. iii, 11. But the Law was of some service to them, in that it furnished a check upon idolatry and immorality, and thus as a schoolmaster, it *prepared* them for Christ and the new covenant.—Gal. iii, 19, and iv, 1.

The Law Covenant was ordained in the hands of a mediator—*Moses;* and that covenant and its mediator were a *shadow*, or type of the future "*New* covenant" and its mediator—Christ. Moses *typically bought* all Israel with the blood of the bullock and goat, which typically represented his own blood—life. He typically bought them and left them the conditions of the Law as a *legacy*. For a covenant is of force after men (the ratifiers or mediators) are dead.... "When Moses had spoken every precept to all the people, according to the Law, he took the blood of bulls and of goats, with water and scarlet wool and hyssop, and sprinkled both the book—(the Law)—and all the people, saying: this is the blood of the covenant which God hath enjoined unto you."—Heb. ix, 16-20. When Jesus came he was born into the world—"under the Law," and by perfect obedience to it he became the heir of all the earthly promises contained in that Law covenant—but more, he was begotten of God and was *the Seed* of Abraham, and as such was heir of the *first* covenant also. —Gal. iii, 16. In the person of Jesus then, the second (Law) covenant passed away, *being fulfilled:* and the first—(Abrahamic)—covenant *began* to be fulfilled: for it will not be completely fulfilled until "all families of the earth" are *blessed* by Christ.

This blessing of mankind is made the basis of a "*New Covenant*" between God and man. This, like the "Law" covenant, has conditions, some of which bind God and some bind mankind. Mankind will be required to keep God's perfect *Law*. [He could not give an imperfect one—the Law given to Israel was "*holy and just and good.*"—Rom. vii, 12.] Any other Law would be unjust and bad then; consequently, God must give in substance the same Law which Jesus said was briefly comprehended in this: "Thou shalt love the Lord thy God with all thy heart, with all thy mind, with all thy soul, and with all thy strength, and thy neighbor as thyself." So far as man's *obligations* are concerned then, they will be the same under the "*New*" that they were under the Law covenant; the difference consisting in this, that under the "*New*" God will *actually* take away man's sins instead of *typically* (as under the Law.) When God actually takes man's sins away and its penalties (mental and physical imperfections and death) then, and not until then, will they as *perfect men* be able to keep God's perfect Law.

"Behold the days come, saith the Lord, that I will make a *New Covenant* with the house of Israel and with the house of Judah... This shall be the covenant that I will make with the house of Israel after those days, saith the Lord: I will put my law in their inward part and write it in their hearts, and I will be their God and they shall be my people, for I will forgive their iniquity, and I will remember their sin no more." "In *those days* they shall say no more, the fathers have eaten a sour grape, and the children's teeth are set on edge, but every one shall die for his own iniquity."—Jer. xxxi, 29. "And in *that day*, I will make a covenant for them with the beasts of the field and with the fowl of heaven, and with the creeping things of the ground, and I will break the bow and the sword and the battle out of the earth."—Hos. ii, 18. See also Jer. xxxii, 37-41; Ezek. xxxvii, 12, 14, 26. It may easily be seen that these conditions are not yet fulfilled. The sour grape of *sin* still sets all mankind on edge—the law of sin, the stony heart, still remains in mankind:

God has not yet taken it away and given them instead a heart of flesh (perfect manhood) with his law—*Love*—graven thereon. The beasts and fowl are not yet in harmony with man. He was given dominion, glory, and honor, but through sin lost it almost entirely; but soon he will be restored, and all nature will recognize in man her ruler. But it may be asked—Upon what conditions will God take away and blot out man's transgressions? We answer, *unconditionally:* according to the provisions of the first covenant, a *seed* was to come, and secondly it was to *bless all*. The blessing is the removal of man's load of sin, through the death of the seed, who died the just for the unjust. This (third) "New Covenant" like its shadow, the Law, has a mediator, because there are conditions, and two parties to the covenant. As under the Law Covenant Moses was the mediator, so is

"JESUS THE MEDIATOR OF THE NEW COVENANT,"

and to him God looks for the fulfillment of the Law; and to him Israel and the world look for *ability* to comply with its conditions, viz., restitution. As the mediator, or *testator* then, Jesus must *die* to leave mankind the legacy—of forgiveness and restoration promised in the New Covenant. He did thus die and bought all with his own precious blood, and soon is to commence the great work of applying the blood—cleansing from all sin. As typically Moses took the bunch of hyssop and scarlet wool, and therewith sprinkled of the ratifying blood both the book (Law) and all the people, (Heb. ix, 19,) so with the New Covenant, it must be ratified with *blood*, and the mediator gives his blood (life) and then (*soon* we believe) he will begin the work of sprinkling with this cleansing blood and with the pure water of truth. He will sprinkle both the book (Law) and people, bringing the people into harmony with God's law— "*Love.*" No longer will their teeth be set on edge; no longer will they, when they would do good, find evil present with them; then, all shall know the Lord from the least to the greatest, and the knowledge of the Lord shall fill the whole earth.

But does some one inquire why the new covenant did not at once go into effect as soon as the mediator died? Why were not all the people sprinkled as soon as the blood was shed?

Ah! dear friends, that is the most wonderful part of it all: that is the part which shows "the *exceeding riches* of God's grace"— "his loving-kindness toward *us, in Christ.*" This is what Paul repeatedly speaks of, as the "*mystery*" hid during previous ages, viz., "Christ in you the hope of *glory.*"—Col. i, 27. Jesus died for and is to bless and restore all men; but before entering upon the work of restoring, he publishes among the great mass (all of whom he ransomed) the news of their ransom, and to all who have an ear to hear it he extends the *privilege* of taking up their cross and following him—of sharing with him in suffering evil for good, and promises these that if they do walk in his footsteps they shall be not only sharers of the sufferings, but also of the "*glory* that shall follow." "To him that overcometh will I grant to sit with me in my throne." We shall become heirs of God, joint-heirs with Jesus Christ our Lord, if so be that we suffer with him, that we may be also glorified together."—Rom. viii. 17.

This is the reason why the Gospel age intervenes between the death of Jesus and the blessing of the world: it is an age of death, an age during which we *may* if we will—"fill up what is behind of the afflictions of Christ."—Col. i, 24. We are then, joined with Christ in the sacrifice of the human life—"*dead with him*," and so far as the world is concerned, they are still waiting until the little flock—the members of the body of the mediator or testator (Christ) are "dead with him." We believe the sacrifice to be almost ended, and soon all who have shared death with him as *members of his body* shall be joined with him in the glory of power and share in the glorious work of applying the blood—cleansing the people. Moses did the sprinkling in the type and it will be the Great Prophet and Mediator in the antitype. "A prophet shall the Lord your God raise up unto you of your brethren, like unto me; him shall ye hear in all things whatsoever he shall say unto you. And it shall come to pass that every soul which will not hear that prophet, shall be destroyed from among the people."—Acts iii, 22. This prophecy belongs to the "times of restitution of all things," and is quoted by Peter as applicable there.

That prophet, or teacher—"the Christ"—head and body, is now being "raised up" (to power), and soon the work of sprinkling and cleansing humanity begins; and the soul (person) who will not then obey and be cleansed shall be destroyed. In that age, the sinner a hundred years old will be cut off, though at that age he would be but "a child."—Isa. lxv, 20.

In a sense, the operation of the *new* covenant begins with the Gospel church, and lifts us from the plane of degradation and sin to a justified or *reckoned perfect* condition, from which we can go forward in the "narrow way" becoming heirs of the *first* covenant.—Gal. iii, 29. Let us briefly review these covenants as they are illustrated in a type or allegory.—(Gal. iv, 22-31). Paul explained that Abraham's wife, Sarah, was a type of the *first* covenant made with Abraham, referring to "the Seed." As years rolled by, and no child came, they began to look for a fulfillment in some other way, and Hagar takes the place of a wife and bears a son, who apparently is to be the *heir*. So the original promise of God meant Christ, but he was not born until "due time," and in the meantime "the Law" was given from Sinai, apparently taking the place of *the first* covenant, and under the law covenant a *fleshly seed* was developed—fleshly Israel. But the first, or Sarah, covenant had not failed, and after the Hagar covenant had borne fleshly Israel (typified by Ishmael), the true seed of Abraham and heir is born, under the *first* (or Sarah) covenant; *i. e.*, Christ Jesus and the members of his body—spiritual Israel. This is as far as Paul carries the type, because speaking only of the two *seeds*, natural and spiritual, and the two covenants under which they come into existence. But as we find that God is to make "*a new* covenant," "after those days," we naturally inquire: Why was not this *new* covenant typified by a wife as well as the other two? And upon examination we find it was so illustrated. Turning to Gen. xxiv, 67, we read how Isaac receives Rebecca into Sarah's tent, and she becomes his married wife, (illustrating how our heavenly Bridegroom will receive his Bride at the end of her journey, and bring her into possession of and associate her with himself, in the enjoyment of all things promised in the first (or Sarah) covenant.) Then we read *after* Isaac's marriage: "*Then, again*, Abraham took a wife, and her name was Keturah," thus illustrating as plainly as a type can, the "*New* covenant."

Each of the first two covenants bore but *one* offspring. The first, the "heir of all things," (Christ Jesus and we his Bride,) and the second, fleshly Israel, beloved for the Fathers' sake. But the New Covenant (Keturah) bears six sons, which, taken with the one of Hagar, would be *seven*—a complete number—representing that all the fleshly children would be developed under the Hagar and Keturah, or "Law" and "New" Covenants.

The name Sarah means *Princess;* Hagar means *flight* or *cast out;* Keturah means *incense* or *sweet;* all of which are significant. Oh, how our covenant—the Royal—looms up above all the others! Let us not forget that we must *die* with Jesus if we would LIVE and share in the glorious work of sprinkling and cleansing the world in the next age. "That by means of *death* . . . they which are called might receive the promise of *eternal* inheritance."—Heb. ix, 15.

PART X.

AN EXPLANATION OF SOME SCRIPTURES FREQUENTLY MISCONSTRUED.

THE RICH MAN AND LAZARUS.

This parable recorded in Luke xvi, 19, is generally regarded as being the utterance of our Lord (though nothing is said of his having uttered it), and we so regard it.

The great difficulty with many is, that though they call it a parable, they reason on it, and draw conclusions from it, as though it were a literal statement and not a parable. To think of it as a *literal statement* involves quite a number of absurdities; for instance: that the *rich man* went to hell because he had enjoyed many earthly blessings and gave nothing but crumbs to Lazarus. Not a word is said about his wickedness. Again, Lazarus is blessed, not because he is a sincere child of God, full of faith and trust—not because he was *good*, but simply because he was *poor and sick*. If this be understood literally, the only logical lesson to be drawn from it is, that unless you are a poor beggar, full of sores, you will never enter into future bliss, and if now you wear any *"fine linen"* and *"purple,"* and have plenty to eat *every day*, you are sure to go to hades. Again, the place of bliss is "Abraham's *bosom*," and if the whole statement is literal, the *bosom* must be literal, and would not hold very many of earth's millions of sick and poor. But why consider the absurdities? All unprejudiced minds recognize it as a parable.

As a parable, how shall we understand it? We answer, that a parable is *one thing said, another thing meant;* we know this from some of the parables explained by Jesus. For instance, the parable of the "Wheat and Tares." From his explanation we learn that when in that parable he said *wheat*, he meant "children of the kingdom;" when he said *tares*, he meant (to those who would understand the parable) "the children of the devil;" when he said *reapers*, angels were to be understood, etc. (See Matt. xiii.) So you will find it in every parable *explained* by our Lord; the *thing said* is never the *thing meant;* consequently in this parable "a rich man" means something else. Lazarus and Abraham's bosom are not literal, but represent some class and condition. In attempting to expound a parable such as this, an explanation of which our Lord does not furnish us, modesty in expressing our *opinions* regarding it is certainly appropriate. We therefore offer the following explanation without any attempt to force our view upon the reader, except so far as his own truth-enlightened judgment may commend them, as in accord with God's Word and plan. To our understanding "the rich man" represented the Jewish nation. At the time of the utterance of the parable, and for a long time previous, they had "fared sumptuously every day"—being the especial recipients of God's favors. As Paul says: "What advantage then hath the *Jew?* Much every way; chiefly, because to them was committed the oracles of God."—[Law and Prophesy.] The promises to Abraham and David invested this people with *royalty*, as represented by the rich man's "*purple*." The ritual and (typical) sacrifices of the Law constituted them, in a *typical* sense, a holy nation—righteous—represented by the rich man's "fine linen." [Fine linen is a symbol of righteousness.—Rev. xix, 9.]

Lazarus represented the Gentiles—all nations of the world aside from the Israelites. These, at the time of the utterance of this parable, were entirely destitute of those blessings which Israel enjoyed; they lay at the gate of the rich man. No rich promises of royalty were theirs; not even typically were they cleansed; but in moral sickness, pollution, and sin they were companions of "dogs." Dogs were regarded as detestable creatures in those days, and the typically clean Jew called the outsiders "heathen" and "dogs," and would never eat with them, nor marry nor have any dealings with them.—John iv, 9. As to the "eating the crumbs (of favor) which fell from the rich man's table" of bounties, Jesus' words to the Syro-Phœnician woman give us a key. He said to this Gentile woman—"It is not meet (proper) to take the children's (Israelites) bread and give it to the dogs" (Gentiles); and she answered, "Yea, Lord, but the dogs eat of the crumbs that fall from their master's table."—Matt. xv, 27. Jesus healed her daughter, thus giving the desired crumb of *favor*. But there came a time when the typical righteousness ceased—when the promise of royalty ceased to be theirs, and the kingdom was taken from them to be given to a nation bringing forth the fruits thereof.—Matt. xxi, 43. The *rich man* died to all these special advantages and soon he (the Jewish nation) found himself in "*gehenna fire*"—a cast-off condition, in trouble, tribulation and affliction, in which they have suffered from that day to this.

Lazarus also died: the condition of the Gentiles underwent a change, and from the Gentiles many were carried by the angels (messengers, apostles, etc.) to Abraham's bosom. Abraham is represented as the father of the *faith-full* and receives to his bosom all the children of faith—who thus are recognized as the heirs to all the promises made to Abraham. For the children of the *flesh*, these are not the children of God, but the "children of the promise are counted for the *seed*" (children of Abraham) "which seed is Christ," and "if ye be Christ's then are ye (believers) Abraham's seed (children) and heirs according to the (Abrahamic) promise."—Gal. iii, 29. Yes, the condition of things then existing terminated by death—at the death of Jesus—"for if one died for all, then were all dead." There the Jew was cast off and has since been shown "no favor," and the poor Gentiles who before had been "aliens from the commonwealth (the promises) of Israel and *without God* and *having no hope* in the world," were then "brought nigh by the blood of Christ", and "reconciled to God."—Eph. ii, 13. If the two tribes living in Judea (Judah and Benjamin) were represented by *one* rich man, would it not be in harmony to suppose that the *five* brethren represented the remaining *ten* tribes, who had "Moses and the Prophets" as their instructors? The question relative to them was doubtless introduced to show that all *special* favor of God ceased to the ten tribes, as well as to the two directly addressed. It seems to us *evident*, that Israel only was meant, for *none other nation* than Israel had "Moses and the prophets" as instructors.

In a word, this parable seems to teach precisely what Paul explained in Rom. xi, 19-31. How that because of unbelief, the natural branches were broken off, and the wild branches grafted in to the Abrahamic promises. In the parable, Jesus leaves them in the trouble, and does not refer to their final restoration to favor, doubtless because it was not pertinent to the feature of the subject treated; but Paul assures us, that when the fullness of the Gentiles—the Bride—be come in "they (the Israelites) shall obtain mercy through your (the Church's) mercy." He assures us that this is God's covenant with *fleshly Israel* (they lost the higher—spiritual—promises, but are still the possessors of certain earthly promises) to become the chief nation of earth, etc. In proof of this statement, he quotes the Prophets, saying: "The deliverer shall come out of Zion, (the glorified church,) and shall turn away ungodliness from *Jacob*," (the fleshly seed). As concerning the Gospel, (high calling) they are enemies, (cast off) for your sakes: but as touching the election, they are beloved for the fathers' sakes. "For God hath concluded them all in unbelief,-that he might have mercy upon all. O the depths of the riches both of the wisdom and knowledge of God!"—Rom. xi, 30-32.

HAVING A DESIRE TO DEPART AND BE WITH CHRIST.

Paul was a prisoner at Rome, awaiting freedom or death, he knew not which. He had, since entering the ministry, gone through an eventful career and endured much suffering. He recounts to the Philippian church that, though he has suffered much, it has resulted in the furtherance of the gospel. Therefore he rejoices. Then he muses, wondering whether it is the will of God that he continue to live, preach, write, and suffer, and thus be a blessing to the church, or whether he has done his work and will rest in death, being at the same time an illustrious *martyr*. And he asks himself, as it were, the question: Which would you prefer to do if it were left to your decision? and concludes that he would not know which of the *two things* to choose; but he knows of a third thing which he would be in *no doubt* about if he were at liberty to choose it. He is in a strait between *two*, having a desire for the third.

The "Emphatic Diaglott" translates the passage thus: "Christ will be magnified in my body by *life* or by *death*. Therefore for me to live is Christ, and to die is gain. But if to live in the flesh, this to me is a fruit of labor; and what I should choose I do not exactly know: I am indeed hard pressed by the *two* things. I have an earnest desire for the RETURNING and being with Christ, since it is very much to be preferred."—Phil. i, 23.

An explanatory foot-note says, relative to the Greek *Analusia*, rendered *returning*, as above: *Analusia*, or the *returning*, being what Paul earnestly desired, could not be death or dissolution, as implied by the word *depart* in common version, because it seemed a matter of indifference to him which of the two—*life* or *death*—he should choose; but he longed for the *analusia*, which was a *third* thing, and very much to be preferred to either of the other *two* things alluded to. The word *analusia* occurs in Luke xii, 36, and is there rendered *return*. "Be you like men waiting for their master when he will *return*," etc.

PART XI.

COUNTING THE COST. HOW MUCH WILL YOU GIVE?

DEAR friends we are not going to pass around the contribution box now, but thinking this to be an all-important question, one upon which depends, perhaps, as much the interest of every one of us, as any question we could propound, let us each for himself carefully consider—How much will you give for the gospel of Christ? But do you say, is it not a *free* gospel? Does not the prophet say "Ho, every one that thirsteth come ye to the waters, and he that has no money come ye, buy, and eat; yea, buy wine and milk *without money* and without price?" Yes, that is a correct *quotation*, but there is nothing in the passage quoted to indicate that a man who *has* money can have the gospel and still *keep* his money; those who are to have it without money are those who *have no money to pay*. But sincerely, my brother, my sister, my friend, HOW MUCH will you give for the gospel? It is *exceedingly* valuable and you should not expect to get it for *nothing*, you should not be willing to take it for nothing if you *could*, neither can you expect to give an *equivalent* for it, for "its price is beyond *rubies*, and all the things thou canst desire are not to be *compared* unto it."

Now if you have some faint idea of its value, perhaps you will be willing to make some *offer* for it. Offerings are in order for it *now*, this is "the acceptable (receivable) year of the Lord," and we are close to "the day of vengeance of our God;" and if you want a chance in the high calling, you need to be quick and prompt about it; we expect the quota under this call will soon be filled, and hope you will not be among the number who will "stand without knocking and saying open unto us," when it will be *forever too late*. Again we ask, How *much* will you *give*?

Suppose we consider the word *give* first in the sense of *yielding*, "give ear," are you willing to give your *attention* and *thought* to this gospel? Are you willing to bend your mind to it? Are you willing to *carefully, prayerfully* and *persistently* consider it? Are you willing to give it all the thought which you have hitherto given to matters of little or no importance? Consider it well; think of the hours you have spent reading works of fiction, wit and humor, perhaps in playing some sort of *game* for diversion, or even in reading history or secular news, *mainly* for the purpose of being considered "well informed," or possibly for the purpose of being qualified for some position of honor (worldly) or fame. Are you willing to give way, to give that attention to the gospel that you have to these? Do you answer in the affirmative? That is well so far, but that is *not enough*. Are you willing (notice, these questions are for you to answer to yourself in the present tense, *not to-morrow*) to give in the sense of *quitting;* are you willing if this gospel requires it, to give place to principles which will antagonize those which you have hitherto entertained? Are you willing to have a radical change made in your *mind*, and in your manner of reasoning, *i. e.*, so that instead of reasoning from an earthly or natural standpoint, it shall be from a spiritual or *gospel* standpoint? Earthly wisdom would reason, "if thine *enemy* hunger let him starve," and everything else on the same line, but heavenly wisdom *waits* to have our heavenly Father who understands all the weaknesses of our natures, and all the influences that have been brought to bear upon us, adjust matters *for us*, instead of taking them into our own hands and managing from an earthly plane, and with earthly wisdom; that is to say, looked at from an earthly standpoint, we resign, our own wisdom and become fools for Christ's sake. You think that is giving considerable do you? Well it is, but you cannot become a vessel fit for the master's use *without*. Are you willing? Yes. Very well, that is good, but that is *not enough*, for this gospel very likely will reveal to you that very many things which you have hitherto considered harmless in their nature are really very injurious to you, and you will be called upon to give in the sense of *abandoning*, *i. e.*, to let go of in the sense of never taking hold again—a long good-by—to the things you once loved; among them may be earthly hopes and expectations; this heavenly wisdom will teach you that all these are transitory and vain, and that the more you depend upon them the more you will be deceived by them, and the greater will be your disappointment, for your expectations will fail to be realized, and your hopes will be blasted. You will find everything turned around under the influence of the gospel, and that the things which are highly esteemed among men are abominations in the sight of God.—Luke xvi, 15. Notice the words "*highly* esteemed among men;" earthly things needful for our physical well-being are not to be despised, nor will heavenly wisdom prompt us to despise them, nor are *they* the things referred to as highly esteemed among men, for men will sacrifice these for worldly honor and wealth. If you will *give way* to the influences of the gospel upon you, you will be led to abominate that which is HIGHLY esteemed among men.

Let us see *what* things are highly esteemed among men; what do they make the greatest sacrifice for? Probably the *greatest* effort that men make is to be *worshipped;* honor, fame, a *name* among men; not so much to *be* superior as to be *regarded* superior. To have men cast out your *name as evil*, that is a terrible thing for a man who knows nothing of the gospel of Christ; to lose his *reputation* is *one* of the greatest, if not *the* greatest, calamity that can befall a man; he will not mind as much the loss of his *character*, but the loss of his *reputation* is most terrible to the man of the world, for if you lose *this* you will lose your worldly friends *mostly;* some of them will stand by if you have plenty of *money*, but it will take a great deal even of money to hold many friends after your reputation is all gone: so if you relinquish your reputation *for the sake* of the gospel (*nothing else* should induce a man to part with it) you will be doing pretty well, you will be *giving* considerable. Do you think you can do it? Y-e-s? Well, can you not say it with emphasis? "By the grace of God I will!" That is *good*. You are giving yourself poor, after the wisdom of this world, arn't you? Never mind, look not at the things that are seen; they are *temporal*. But you have *not given enough* yet—Have you any money? (No, we are not going to pass the contribution box now.) Yes, some. Well much or little you will need to give it, not to pay for the gospel, but out of gratitude and that it may be sent to *others*, and there are some of the Lord's brethren living near your house that are hungry or sick and need help, so your (?) money will be needed, and with it will go those few friends who stuck by you for your *money's* sake after your reputation was gone; you found by bitter (blessed) experience that a great share of your friends left you when your reputation did, and *now* the rest of your worldly friends will go and you will be left alone. Will you do it? "Yes, by the grace of God I will!" The sting of death (to the world) is past, isn't it? How much easier it is to say yes, now. Praise the Lord! But you have not *given enough* yet.

Now, my dear friend, you are not far from the kingdom. Will you sacrifice your ease, your comfort, yea, *life* itself if called upon? Will you let it be worn out, or burnt out, or in any way *used up* for the sake of the gospel of Christ? You will? Thank God! I am *so glad;* you will be *so rich*. Now let us look over this covenant. You have given your attention, your time, your mind, your reputation, your friends, your money, your *life—seven* items. You have given yourself *poor* indeed, haven't you? I acknowledge the fact: *it is so*, poor, *very* poor, and you have done this *willingly*. It makes me think of something I have heard, and while I am looking at you your countenance seems *changed;* you remind me of *some one* I have known. Ah, it comes to me now! *Jesus of Nazareth* was his name; why, *how much* you *resemble* him; you must be his *brother*. "You know the *grace* of our Lord Jesus Christ, that though he *was* rich, yet for our sakes he became poor, that we through his poverty might be rich."—II Cor. viii, 9. Why, you have done just as *he* did and just what he intended when he said: "I have given you an example that ye should do as I have done to you."—John xiii, 15. Well, that is the best kind of will you could make, and I am glad to greet you as *my brother;* I also having done the same things—"for which cause *he* is not ashamed to call *us brethren*." —Heb. ii, 11. You can afford to be poor and go about in disguise for awhile, now, inasmuch as you are an heir of the kingdom. "Hearken, my beloved brethren, hath not God chosen the poor of this world, rich in faith, and heirs of the kingdom which he hath promised to them that love him?"—James ii, 5. And now you will *learn* faster and be able to prepare yourself for regal employment in the royal family; for "if any man will (wills or *wishes* to) do his will, he shall *know* of the doctrine."— John vii, 17. You now belong to that company so aptly described by the poet when he said:

> "What poor despised company
> Of travelers are these,
> Who walk in yonder narrow way,
> Along the rugged maze?

> "Ah, these are of a royal line,
> All children of a *King*,
> Heirs of immortal crowns divine,
> And lo, for joy they sing!

"Why do they, then, appear so m[ean]
And why so much despised?
Because of their rich robes unse[en]
The world is not apprized!

"But why keep they that narrow [way]
That rugged, thorny maze?
Why, that's the way their leader [trod]
They love and keep his ways.

"What! is there, then, no other r[oad]
To Salem's happy ground?
Christ is the only way to God;
None other can be found."

"ASK AND YE SHALL RECEIVE[."]

To as many as have carefully read this little pamp[hlet and] become deeply interested in the subjects as herein pre[sented,] we would say: If you want further reading-matter on these sub-jects, write to us. If you are desirous of having preaching on these glorious themes, let us know, and we will endeavor to have the want supplied. If you want some of

These Pamphlets Free for your Friends,

whom you think would be interested in reading them, write, stating how many you can use judiciously.

We expect to issue soon a FREE TRACT, entitled, "THE TABERNACLE AND ITS TEACHINGS:"—Ask and ye shall receive.

Address, **"ZION'S WATCH TOWER,"**

No. 101 Fifth Avenue, Pittsburgh, Pa., U. S. A.

www.ingramcontent.com/pod-product-compliance
Lightning Source LLC
Chambersburg PA
CBHW030251170426
43202CB00009B/699